HISPANIC CUSTOMERS FOR LIFE

A Fresh Look at Acculturation

M. Isabel Valdés

Paramount Market Publishing, Inc.

Paramount Market Publishing, Inc.
950 Danby Road, Suite 136
Ithaca, NY 14850
www.paramountbooks.com
Telephone: 607-275-8100; 888-787-8100 | Facsimile: 607-275-8101

Publisher: James Madden
Editorial Director: Doris Walsh

Library of Congress Catalog Number:
Cataloging in Publication Data available
ISBN 978-0-9786602-6-0

To the pioneers of Hispanic Marketing

Contents

Acknowledgments

Like my previous books, this book is comprehensive and rich in insights thanks to the contributions of many people. First and foremost, my publishing team extraordinaire, who patiently waited, contributed, coached, and supported me while I pondered what was the *right book* for the new Hispanic marketing times, a process that took over two years! I am blessed to count them among my strongest supporters and friends. Thanks Doris and Jim, Anne, and Tobi!

To Charlie Veraza, Lindsay Daigle and Marissa Jarratt, Richard Montañez (Frito-Lay,) and Dieste, Harmel &Partners for developing the comprehensive integrated marketing case study of the Hispanic Sunflower Initiative; I appreciate "de corazón" your time, effort and dedication it took to make this real-life example available, gracias! Needless to say, the inclusion of this and previous PepsiCo case studies would not be possible without the blessings and support of Frito-Lay's and PepsiCo's senior management, specially, Steve Reinemund, (former CEO) who brought passion and commitment to the Inclusion/Diversity strategies, leading by example; to PepsiCo's current CEO, Indra Nooyi and her trailblazing commitment "to positive intent" elevating this commitment to new heights; to Al Carey, Frito-Lay's present CEO, Al Bru, (past CEO,) to PepsiCola CEO, Dawn Hudson and Ron - "Roncito" Parker, Senior V.P., PepsiCO's visionary HR guru! It is not by chance Wall Street has witnessed such great performance from this global giant. Their leadership and 360-degree holistic approach has paid off! Thanks for your support and generosity.

To my dear friend Norma Orci. I am honored to publish for the first time the definition of the *Share of Heart* philosophy that she created and brought to the advertising trade over three decades ago—not only the Hispanic marketing and advertising world—but around the globe. Norma, you are a marketing genius! We owe you big time for opening the doors to of a new age of honest, emotional, and compassionate advertising! Also thanks to Hector Orci for updating Honda's Case study one more time; this case study is probably the first and most successful holistic and longitudinal Hispanic marketing and advertising strategy in US Hispanic marketing history! And the first ever *Share of Heart* marketing and advertising strategy that continues to bring billions in ROI to Honda of America. Many thanks to Honda of Americas' senior management, especially Eric Conn, for their foresight and generosity by providing access to their business strategy for a decade to help train future generations of successful Hispanic marketers. I'm highly indebted to your investment in deep psychographic research, never cutting corners! This allowed me at HMC, Inc. to develop, test and track the value of the *Share of Heart* philosophy in action and develop the first multi-dimensional psychographic models and segmentation for Hispanic marketing. Thanks for your faith in my "novel and unusual" research models!

Thanks to: many clients, friends and colleagues, and pioneers in Hispanic marketing who have shared their insights for this and previous books with their case studies, as well as my friend and colleague Terry Soto, for her support in the early stages of this book and contributions. Many thanks to Carlos Santiago, Monica Talan, Marta Montoya (author of *Los Kitos*), Raul Lopez, Eva May, Victoria Varela, Tom Maney, Carl Kravetz, Lorraine Yglesias, and Hank Armstrong. I could not have produced these books without their commitment and dedication.

I am also indebted to colleagues that contributed to the book with their personal experiences, books, papers, reviews and advice, David Hayes Bautista, Ph.D., Federico A. Subervi-Velez, Ph.D., (particularly for his seminal work on Latino "Situational Latinidad and Identity") to Lionel Sosa, Kirk Whisler, Angel Chavez, Macuqui Robau-Garcia, Maria Contreras Sweet, Peter Bellas, Tom Exter, Monica Lozano Ph.D., Neil Comber, Derene Allen, Horacio Gomes, Dolores Valdés Creel, Xavier Saucedo, Jannet Torres, Michael Caplinger, Marcos Baer, Dolores Kunda, Efrain Fuentes, Ph.D., and Jake Beniflah (Ph.D. candidate).

Special thanks to Richard Ventura, President of the San Francisco Hispanic Chamber of Commerce, for demonstrating how grassroots organizations can partner with clients to reach the community. (See VISA Case Study, p.)

Very special thanks to Anita Santiago and our ASA team members! Ingrid Otero Smart, Lloyd Lopez, Letha Davis, Sofia Escamilla, Peter Brawn, and Creative Director Francisco Letelier

Without the wealth of data provided by colleagues, friends and their organizations, I would not be able to bring to you the segmentation and analysis in this book. They are pioneers in marketing to Latinos and generous with their data; Arturo Villar, (*Hispanic Market Weekly*,) and Jesus Chavarria, (*Hispanic Business Magazine*), Marcela Medina, Ceril Shagrin, Beth Bachrach, Debbie Shinnick, (Univision,) Cesar Melgoza, (Geoscape). To Harry Pachon, (Tomas Rivera Institute), Jim Estrada, (HCM/Latino Initiative Report), Eugenio (Gene) Bryan, (HispanicAd.com), Robert B. Textor, Meredith Spector and Michelle Zweig, (AC Nielsen Hispanic Panel,) and to Marta H. Seoane, Ph.D., co-author of my first book (*The Hispanic Market Handbook*, 1995, Gale Research Publishers).

Many thanks to Sylvia Flores, founder of *www.Click2Latino.com*, for updating and compiling the present on-line resources section. To Chris Ferejohn, who typed innumerable versions of the book's manuscript, provided editorial suggestions.

Last, but certainly not least, many thanks to my dear children, Gabriel Aranovich, M.D. and Clarita Aranovich, who took time from their busy lives to help with the editing, typing, and support for mom's new book. I will always cherish the fun hours spent together preparing "Zee New Book!" and to my mentors and advisors, Raul Yzaguirre, Irma Flores (Q.E.P.D.) and Arabella Martinez.

Gracias !
M. ISABEL VALDÉS
San Francisco, CA
October 2007

Preface

HISPANICS, like other immigrant groups in the past have contributed to the history, culture, and economics of the United States. Those contributions continue today.

Unlike the past, computer technology has made it easier for marketers to learn where these immigrants live, how long they have been in this country, and information about their preferred language. Surveys and customer data give us a great deal of information about their attitudes and lifestyles, likes and dislikes.

As the Hispanic population in the United States continues to grow and prosper, marketers need new ways to target these customers that go far beyond mere demographics. My two books, *Marketing to American Latinos, A Guide to the In-Culture Approach, Parts I and II* (Paramount Market Publishing, 2000 and 2002, respectively) laid out the cultural aspects that differentiate Hispanics from Anglos and provided detailed data on purchasing behavior and segmentation by age.

This book, *Hispanic Customers for Life: A Fresh Look at Acculturation,* segments the Hispanic market by generations in the U.S. This groundbreaking way of describing the U.S. Hispanic market will help marketers, advertisers, non-profit organizations, and policy makers better understand the differences among Hispanics who have recently arrived in the U.S. and those who have been in the country for two or more generations.

The effects of on-going acculturation have created a market that is diverse in its use of media, its family values, its purchase behavior, and more. Once you understand this diversity, you will be well on your way to attracting *Hispanic Customers for Life!*

M. ISABEL VALDÉS
San Francisco, CA
October 2007

CHAPTER 1

U.S. Latinos
From 15+ Percent on to 25+ Percent

Today—Looking into Tomorrow

In May 2007, the official U.S. Census estimate of the U.S. Hispanic population was 45.5 million,[1] representing about 15 percent of the total U.S. population. However, if the 3.9 million U.S. citizens living in Puerto Rico● and the estimated 1.5 million Hispanic population census undercount are added, the true—or effective—size of the U.S. Hispanic market today is over 50 million!

The 2000 Census made it official: the "Sleeping Giant" has awakened! With a surge of 13 million people between 1990 and 2000, Hispanics grew faster than any other ethnic group, a record 58 percent. By contrast, the number of non-Hispanic whites increased by only about 5 percent. Hispanic population growth is projected to continue for the foreseeable future (Figure 1.1).

● THE ISLAND OF PUERTO RICO IS AN UNINCORPORATED TERRITORY OF THE UNITED STATES UNDER A COMMONWEALTH STATUS.

FIGURE 1.1

U.S. Hispanic Population and Projection, 1950–2050*

population in millions

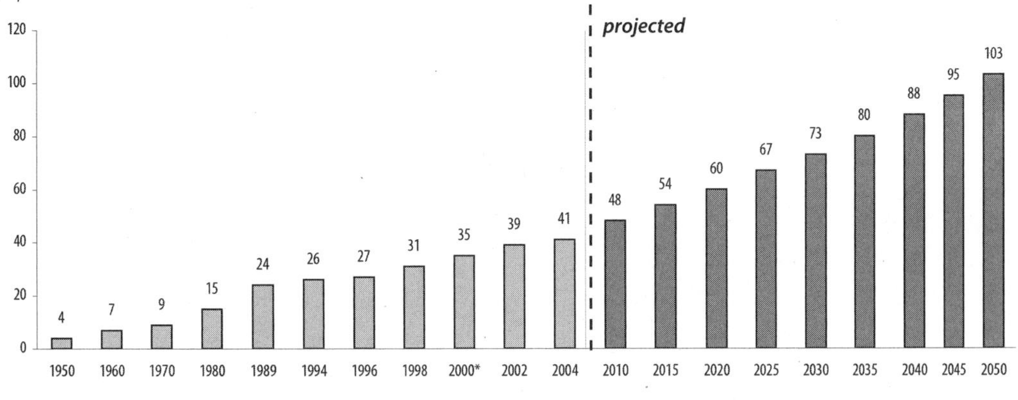

Note: Does not include 3.9 million Puerto Rican Islanders

Source: U.S. Census. The Hispanic Population in the United States, 2004

FIGURE 1.2 ·

U.S. Total Hispanic Population and Selected
Latin American Countries, 2006

COUNTRY	POPULATION (ESTIMATED)
Mexico	108.7 million
United States Hispanics	**49.6 million***
Colombia	45.6 million
Argentina	40.1 million
Peru	27.2 million

*Includes 3.9 million Puerto Rico Islanders and the estimated 1.5 million Census population undercount.

Source: IVC estimates, based on Geoscape International, American Marketscape DataStream, 2006 series http://www.hmw-datacenter.com/marketProfiles.asp?dma=US.

To put this in context, the U.S. Hispanic population has surpassed the total population of major U.S. trading partners such as Australia (21 million) and Canada (32 million), and despite the growing number of bilingual and English-speaking Latinos, U.S. Hispanics are still one of the "largest Spanish-speaking communities in the world." (Figure 1.2)

Hispanic Population Today: The Advent of *Generational Crossover*

The Hispanic market is experiencing the most important socio-demographic shift since its official emergence as a powerful and distinct U.S. market segment. Figure 1.3 summarizes visually the generational paradigm shift taking place in the U.S. Hispanic market today. By 2016, it will be a different market altogether, with the vast majority of 20-to-29-year-old U.S. Hispanics U.S. born. Since the majority of these are born to at least one foreign-born parent, acculturation levels, consumer behavior, language usage, and so forth will still play a role and reflect immigrant assimilation and adaptation gaps. This trend will be more marked among lower-income, less-educated family households.

FIGURE 1.3 ·

Latino Generational Crossover, 2006

foreign-born vs. U.S.-born Hispanic population by age

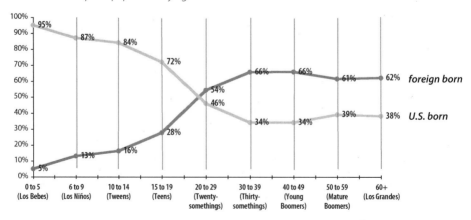

Source: M. Isabel Valdés, 2007 data consistent with independent estimates including those from the Pew Hispanic Center and the Census Bureau's 2006 March Current Population Survey, Annual Social and Economic Supplement.

In contrast, a high percentage of foreign-born Latinos are aging and retiring from the workforce. Many may not be financially prepared for retirement, and will become dependent on their children or the state. There is an urgent need to aggressively pursue and help Latino baby boomers in this regard with targeted educational retirement planning programs. See Chapters 9 and 10 for detailed analysis of the different generation-based, *GenAge Segments*.

FIGURE 1.4

Hispanic Population Distribution by Generation and Age, 2004

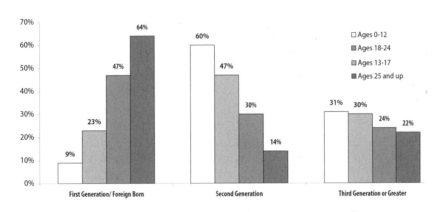

Source: M. Isabel Valdés, 2007, adapted from U.S. Census Current Population Survey, November 2004.

The U.S. Hispanic market, as no other market in history, has grown through several waves of immigrants that have added to the preexisting population, dating back to the descendents of the Spanish colonies and Mexicans who resided in the continental U.S. since the mid-1500s (see Chapter 3).

Reflecting on the most recent waves of Hispanic immigration over the past four decades, these earlier generations of what we call today the "Hispanic" or "Latino"• market grew into generations and sub-generations.

These sub-generations are perhaps the most relevant socio-demographic phenomenon that has impacted Hispanic marketing in the past two decades and it will continue to be so for the foreseeable future.[2]

The latest wave of Hispanic immigrants of the 1970s, 1980s, and 1990s created a distinct Hispanic marketing segment that I have called the "foreign-born" or first generation (G1). Together with their children and grandchildren born in the past 40 years, they have added a large number of Latino consumers to the U.S. born—the second generation (G2) and third generation (G3+) Hispanic

• I USE THE TERMS "HISPANIC" AND "LATINO" INTER-CHANGEABLY. BOTH TERMS ARE COMMONLY USED IN BUSINESS.

market segments. Each of these segments has somewhat distinct demographic and psychographic profiles. Chapters 8, 9, and 10 present data and tools to market to the acculturating Hispanic population.

Hispanic Population Tomorrow

According to Census Bureau projections, over 50 million people of Hispanic origin (who may be of any race) will be added to the nation's population between 2006 and 2050, growing from 44.2 million to 103 million, an estimated increase of 137 percent. Similarly, the Hispanic share of the total U.S. population will nearly double, from 14.5 percent to 24.3 percent, not including Puerto Rico.[3]

Overall, the total U.S. population will continue to grow, increasing from 282.1 million in 2000 to 419.9 million in 2050. However, after 2030 the growth rate might be the slowest since the Great Depression of the 1930s, as the size of the "baby boom" population will continue to decline.[4]

From 2000 to 2050, the white, non-Hispanic population will increase from 195.7 million to 210.3 million, an increase of only 14.6 million or 7 percent. The share of the white, non-Hispanic population is actually expected to decline starting in the 2040s and will comprise just 50.1 percent of the total population by 2050, compared with 69.4 percent in 2000.[5]

By 2030, about one in five U.S. residents will be 65 or older. In contrast, Hispanics will be underrepresented in this age group, and while the population of the U.S. as a whole gets older, the Hispanic population will be young and in their prime productive years.

Projections to 2050

In 2005, the U.S. Census Bureau released population projections for the U.S. to 2050; by then, the Hispanic market is projected to become 25 to 27 percent of the total U.S. population, with well over 100 million people of Latin origin.

The Census data shows Hispanics will continue to be young, productive, and major players in the labor market, with hefty segments of Hispanics in their twenties, thirties, forties, and fifties. These people will be contributing to the economy particularly as consumers, workers in the labor force, and as entrepreneurs and political participants.

FIGURE 1.5 .. ..

Total Hispanic Population Growth Projection by Age Segments, 2005–2050

in millions

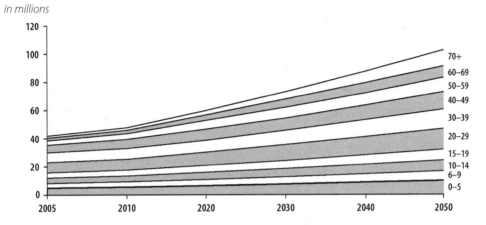

Source: M. Isabel Valdés, 2007, adapted from U.S. Census usproj2000-2050.xls

Latinos: Younger Now, Younger Tomorrow

Latinos are younger, with a median age of just 28 years in 2006 compared with 35.5 years for the total U.S. population. In 2005, 37.5 percent of Hispanics were aged 19 or younger, compared with 24.2 percent of white non-Hispanics.[6] (Figure 1.6)

The fastest growing cohort within the U.S. Hispanic population is the U.S.-born one, which is dramatically younger than any other significant U.S. population segment, with an average age of just 17.

FIGURE 1.6 .. ..

Median Age by Ethnic Group, 2005

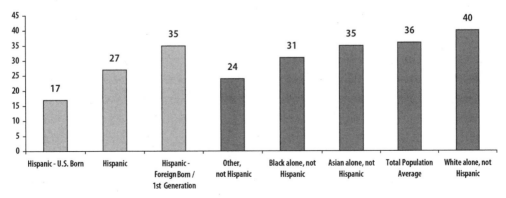

Source: Pew Hispanic Center. Tabulations of 2005 American Community Survey.

Latinos will continue to contribute to the young population in the United States while non-Hispanic whites continue to age. New births continue to increase the young Latino population, whereas the Latino senior population only shows important growth after the years 2040 and 2050.

FIGURE 1.7

Selected Age Groups and Median Age, 2004

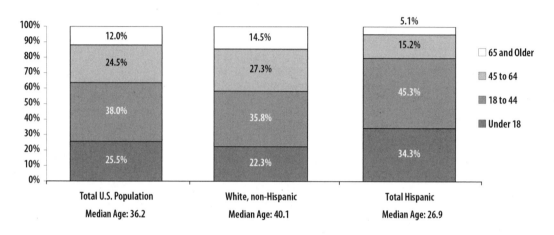

Notes: Data based on sample limited to the household population and exclude the population living in institutions, college dormitories, and other group quarters. For information on confidentiality protection, sampling error, nonsampling error, and definitions, see factfinder.census.gov/home/en/datanotes/exp_acs2004.html. Some percentages do not sum to 100.0 due to rounding.

Source: U.S. Census Bureau. 2004 American Community Survey. Selected Population Profiles, S0201.

From a business perspective, the unprecedented population and economic growth of the Hispanic market is reflected daily in the marketplace. A burgeoning number of Hispanic men, women, and children patronize supermarkets, automotive dealerships, general and specialty stores, banks, amusement parks, clinics and hospitals, and restaurants.

Their presence is being felt not only at the consumer level, but also in the labor market and at the polls. It is also felt in larger numbers in non-traditional Hispanic states and cities. Presently, Latinos can be found in every state of the Union (Figure 1.8) as they continue to relocate within the U.S. wherever job opportunities are available.

FIGURE 1.8 . . . .

Hispanic Household Population by State, 2004

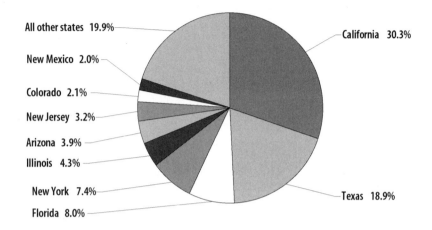

Notes: *Data based on sample limited to the household population and exclude the population living in institutions, college dormitories, and other group quarters. For information on confidentiality protection, sampling error, nonsampling error, and definitions, see factfinder.census.gov/home/en/datanotes/exp_acs2004.html. Some percentages do not sum to 100.0 due to rounding.*

Source: U.S. Census Bureau. 2004 American Community Survey. Selected Population Profiles, S0201.

U.S. Hispanics: Unusual Population Pyramids

A simple way to understand and remember how dramatically different the U.S.-born and foreign-born generations are from one another, as well as from the total U.S. population, is to look at the population pyramids, a great visual tool for comprehending the complexities and differences of the Hispanic population.

FIGURE 1.9 ....

Hispanic Age, Generational, and Gender Distribution

population pyramids for ethnic and nativity groups, 2005

TOTAL HISPANIC

WHITE, NOT HISPANIC

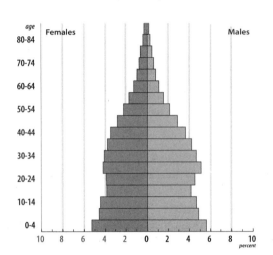

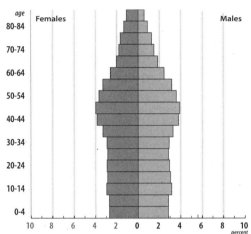

HISPANIC FOREIGN BORN (1ST GENERATION)

HISPANIC U.S. BORN (2ND & 3RD GENERATION)

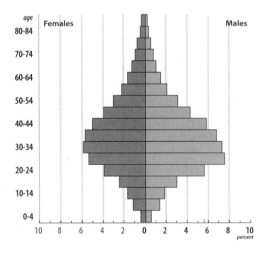

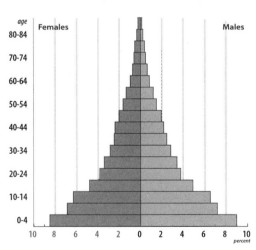

Source: U.S. Census Bureau. 2004 American Community Survey, selected Population Profiles

The vast majority of Latino immigrants leave their home countries as young adults or in their late teens, hence the Latino immigration boom that took place between the 1970s through the late 1990s created a major swell of Latinos who are currently in their mid-20s through mid-40s, as can be seen in Figure 1.9 above in the section labeled Hispanic Foreign Born (1st Generation). It is important to note that many more young men migrated to the U.S., significantly outnumbering foreign-born Hispanic females.

Since the early 2000s, immigration has slowed down. The earlier foreign-born immigrants of the 1970s and 1980s formed families and their children are having children of their own. As a result, foreign-born (1st generation) Latinos are significantly older than the majority of their U.S. born counterparts (2nd and 3rd generations). The social, cultural, and marketing implications of this demographic phenomenon are the center of analysis of this book.

Hispanic Household Growth

Population growth estimates show that Hispanics form over half a million new households each year, contributing to their strength as consumers of all kinds of household goods and services as well as to their visibility among new home-owners and in financial communities. In 2005, someone of Hispanic origin headed more than 12 million households.

FIGURE 1.10 ....

Growth in Hispanic and Non-Hispanic Households, 2000–2005

(in thousands)

	# OF HOUSEHOLDS 2000	# OF HOUSEHOLDS 2005	% CHANGE 2000–2005
Hispanic	9,319	12,181	30.7%
White, non-Hispanic	87,671	92,702	5.7
Black, non-Hispanic	12,849	13,792	7.3
Asian and other	3,337	4,360	30.7
Total households	104,705	113,146	8.1

Source: U.S. Census Bureau. 2006 March Current Population Survey

On average, Hispanic households continue to be larger than non-Hispanic households. In 2004, the Current Population Survey found that 28 percent of Hispanic family households consisted of five or more people. Only 11 percent of non-Hispanic white family households were this large. Family households with only two people represented 24 percent of Hispanic family households, compared with 48 percent of non-Hispanic white households.

Mexican households were most likely to have five or more people, with 33 percent of Mexican family households being this large. Among Hispanic family households, 34 percent of Cuban households had only two people, the largest share of "small households" among all Hispanics. An analysis of the trend shows that overall Hispanic households are becoming smaller, albeit at a much slower pace than non-Hispanic white households.

Hispanic Purchasing Power

The huge economic clout and buying power wielded by Hispanics today, as well as its projected growth, should entice businesses to increase their spending on Hispanic marketing and new business development.

FIGURE 1.11

Projected Evolution of Hispanic Buying Power, through 2010

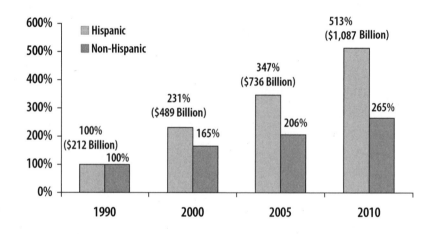

Source: Selig Center for Economic Growth. Terry College of Business, University of Georgia, May 2005

The Selig Center for Economic Growth at the University of Georgia estimates that U.S. Hispanic purchasing power increased dramatically during the 1990s and has continued to rise into the 21st century, from $212 billion in 1990 to $736 billion in 2005, a 347 percent increase over the 15 year period.

Buying power is defined as the total personal (after-tax) income that consumers have to spend on goods and services, or disposable personal income. By 2010, Jeffrey Humphrey, director of the Selig Center, projects Hispanic buying power will top $1 trillion. By 2050, some state the Hispanic consumer market-place "will be worth between $2.5 and $3.6 trillion!"7

Hispanic Income by Household

According to the U.S. Census Bureau, the median household income for Hispanics in 1990 was $30,475. In 2005, the median was $36,000, an 18 percent increase. Personal annual income has risen as well, from $8,424 in 1990 to $12,651 in 2002, to $14,483 in 2005.

FIGURE 1.12 ·

Hispanic Income Growth 1990–2005

	1990	2005
Median Household Income	$30,475	$36,000
Median Personal Income	$8,424	$14,483

Source: U.S. Census Bureau

A breakdown of Hispanic income growth between 2000 and 2005 at the household level as well as the personal income level shows a healthy increase across all income brackets. However, the steepest increase appears in the highest income brackets (Figure 1.13), reflecting the exponential growth in high net-worth Hispanic households (see *High Net-Worth Latinos*, later in this chapter).

The number of households in the lowest income brackets has also increased, but to a lesser extent, suggesting that overall Hispanic households are faring better economically. This also reflects the slowing down in recent immigrant household formation, since historically the majority of recently arrived Hispanic households tend to have lower incomes.

Despite the income growth, it should be noted that 9.4 million Hispanics, 22.6 percent of the Hispanic population, were estimated to be living under the poverty line in 2005; a high percentage of which are probably children.8

FIGURE 1.13 ·

Income Distribution, Hispanic Households, 2000-2005

HOUSEHOLD INCOME	NUMBER OF HISPANIC HOUSEHOLDS (IN 000S)	% OF HISPANIC HOUSE-HOLDS	PERCENT GROWTH 2000–05
100,000+	1,098	8.8%	97.5%
75,000–99,999	1,029	8.2	44.9
50,000–74,999	2,159	17.2	28.4
35,000–49,999	2,141	17.1	25.4
25,000–34,999	1,874	15.0	31.8
15,000–24,999	2,031	16.2	15.1
Under $15,000	2,186	17.5	20.0

Source: U.S. Census Bureau

Hispanic household-income differences exist within the Hispanic market, correlated with country of origin. These differences also can be correlated with the level of educational attainment upon immigration to the U.S. for the majority of immigrants from that country. For example, larger percentages of South Americans and Cubans had college equivalent or professional degrees when they migrated.

Therefore, South American households, comprised of a larger percentage of professional heads of household, continue to have the highest median income ($43,788) followed by Cuban households ($38,256). The lowest median household incomes are found among Dominican immigrants ($29,624).

FIGURE 1.14

Median Household Income by Country of Origin, 2004

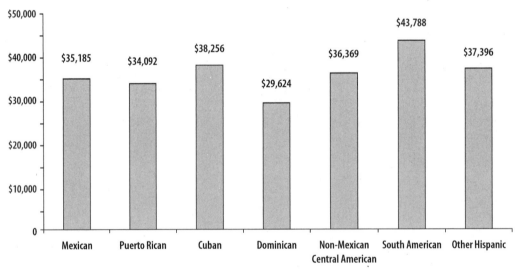

Source: M. Isabel Valdés, based on U.S. Census Bureau, 2004 American Community Survey, selected population profiles.

As Figure 1.15 on page 13 shows, second-generation and third-plus-generations of U.S.-born Hispanic households have greater median incomes than those of foreign-born, first-generation households, according to the 2005 American Community Survey (see previous section on *Hispanic Purchasing Power* for greater detail on this subject).

FIGURE 1.15 . . . .

Median Household Income by U.S.-born/Foreign-born Generation, 2005

HOUSEHOLDS	MEDIAN INCOME
Hispanic	$36,000
U.S. Born (G2, G3+)	$39,000
Foreign Born (G1)	$34,000
U.S. Average	$45,200

Note: Based on reported income, not adjusted income

Source: M. Isabel Valdés, adapted from Pew Hispanic Center tabulations of 2005 American Community Survey.

As the summary table below demonstrates, the Hispanic market represents a lucrative consumer market, composed of a growing number of young Latinos in prime household-formation years, with rapidly growing income potential. Certainly there are "if's" and "how's" to this potential, with access to good education being the greatest hurdle to overcome (see Chapter 4).

FIGURE 1.16 . . . .

Hispanic Income Growth, 1990–2010

	1990	2000	2005	2010
Total U.S. Hispanic Buying Power* (in billions)	$212	$489	$736	$1,087
Household Median Income**	$30,475	$33,447	$35,967	N/A
Personal Annual Median Income**	$8,424	$12,306	$14,483	N/A

*Source: Selig Center for Economic Growth. Terry College of Business, University of Georgia, May 2005
**Source: U.S. Census Bureau

High Net-Worth Latinos

The distribution and growth of Hispanic household income shows a dramatic growth and change between 2000 and 2005. The households in the highest income brackets ($100,000 and up) have almost doubled in five years, and the households making $75,000 to $99,000 have grown by 50 percent (Figure 1.13).

Compared with the total U.S. population, Hispanic households had a higher percentage increase in households with at least $100,000 income between 1980 and 2005 (Figure 1.17).

FIGURE 1.17 ....

Five-Year Growth Rates in $100K Incomes, 1980–2005

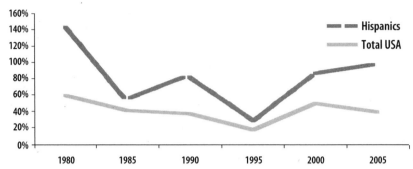

Source: M. Isabel Valdés, adapted from CPS Annual Demographic Survey, U.S. Income Distribution to $250,000 or More for Households, 2000 and 2005 and M. Isabel Valdés, *Capturing the High Net-Worth U.S. Hispanic In-Culture, 2002* (unpublished paper prepared for Merrill Lynch).

High net-worth Hispanic households outnumber high net-worth African-American households, particularly in the highest income brackets (Figure 1.18). As expected, many investment firms are presently pursuing the lucrative Latino household segment.

FIGURE 1.18 ....

Affluent Hispanic and African-American Households, 2005

	HISPANIC	AFRICAN AMERICAN
Total Households	12,519,000	14,002,000
Households with $200K+ annual income*	141,000	120,000
Households with $100K+ net worth**	1,150,000	853,600
Households with $500K+ net worth**	50,000	27,100

*Source: M. Isabel Valdés, adapted from CPS Annual Demographic Survey, U.S. Income Distribution to $250,000 or More for Households, 2005.
**Source: M. Isabel Valdés, *Capturing the High Net-Worth U.S. Hispanic In-Culture, 2002*

As a matter of fact, wealth creation in the Hispanic demographic has fueled an important professional need. There is a major gap in financial services knowledge and financial trust in the Hispanic community. Fortunately for this wealthy Hispanic segment, there are wealth management experts who service them in-culture. These wealth management experts know the unique needs, misgivings, and skeptical attitudes towards money management found among many Hispanics. They also know how to address those fears and concerns. Most significantly, they know what it takes to manage wealth successfully.

CASESTUDY   MERRILL LYNCH

ALIGNING COMMUNITY RESPONSIBILITIES WITH YOUR BUSINESS

Merrill Lynch is committed to being the financial services firm of choice for Hispanic investors in the United States and across the globe. Merrill Lynch has cultivated a presence in local Hispanic communities through its **Investing Pays Off** curriculum—a program focused on helping elementary, middle and high-school students achieve financial literacy. It has created an internal professional network focused on encouraging professional development amongst Hispanic employees.

Merrill Lynch is committed to reflecting the changing face of wealth by building both a diverse client base and a diverse workforce. To demonstrate its commitment to the Hispanic community, Merrill Lynch has aligned with key cultural, professional and philanthropic organizations including The National Council of La Raza, The Tomás Rivera Policy Institute, Museo Del Barrio, and The Museum of Latin American Art (MOLAA).

However, any successful financial services business is the result of successful one-on-one relationships, and Merrill Lynch's senior management is invested in attracting and hiring Latinos for upper-management positions so they can talk to and relate to Latino investors.

Meet wealth-management specialist Angel V. Chavez. His is an exemplary tale of how a Hispanic immigrant from Bolivia rose from the tough streets of the Mission District in San Francisco to become a highly successful financial advisor in Merrill Lynch's San Francisco office.

Angel and his grandmother immigrated to the United States when Angel was five. They lived together in a modest home, taking care of each other. His grandmother worked two or three jobs just to make sure everything went right. She also instilled in Angel the values of education, giving back to the community, and the importance of networking. "My grandmother really planted the seeds of getting a solid education, working hard, and giving back to underserved communities. She emphasized that if I ever made it, not to forget where I came from," said Chavez.

Throughout his childhood, Angel was helped by several Hispanic community organizations and therefore knows the significant role these organizations play in contributing to Hispanic youth. Angel has taken his personal experiences and transformed them into a passion for improving the lives of today's Hispanic youth. One of his recent philanthropic endeavors was with the Latino Community Foundation, which launched a Latino Youth Initiative Fund. The goal of this fund is to promote philanthropic investment in Hispanic children. "There is so much potential among our young people," said Chavez. "Nationally, 41 percent of Latinos drop out of high school. With the rapid population growth of Latinos under the age of 18, it is critical that we get involved **now.** We want this fund to provide grants that build collaboration among organizations for greater impact on youth."

Angel is an active board member of the Latino Community Foundation and the Greater San Jose Hispanic Chamber of Commerce. In addition, he is a member of the Hispanic Association of Realtors and Affiliates and was recently tapped to serve on a selection committee for The United States-Mexico Foundation for the Advancement of Science.

In 2001, Angel joined Merrill Lynch and subsequently founded the Chavez Wealth Management Group. He leads a senior team at Merrill Lynch with more than 50 years of combined wealthmanagement, lending, and private-banking experience. Angel has helped structure significant assets for endowments, foundations, and high-net-worth individuals, and is dedicated to providing clients with a disciplined wealth-management experience. The keys to Angel's business successes are networking and building relationships with members of the Hispanic community. This is aligned with Merrill Lynch's approach to wealth management, which is holistic and relationship-centric. By leveraging the Total Merrill platform, financial advisors like Angel are able to build a partnership with each client that centers on the individual's unique values, aspirations and needs.

Today more than ever the Hispanic community has critical wealth-management needs. Generally speaking, Hispanic small- to mid-size business owners are risk adverse, don't like debt, and are generally mistrusting of institutions. Angel works to dispel those fears. "You see, my business is all relationship-driven. I provide educational seminars that touch on various topics, such as communicating the ten most common mistakes when starting an IRA. This allows me to gain the trust and confidence of people in the community," said Chavez. In turn, this puts Angel in a strong position to earn their business when they grow their assets.

Angel adds value by delivering financial-management education to the Hispanic community. The opportunity is ripe. The supply in the Hispanic market is huge; high-end wealth is growing significantly in the Hispanic community. Angel, along with Merrill Lynch, recognizes this opportunity—**Hispanic Market Demographics** show the buying power of Hispanics is projected to reach $1.87 billion by 2010. For Angel, now more than ever, things are paying off for his business because of the relationship cultivation he has undertaken.

Different States, Different Incomes

Purchasing power and household income varies by state. The Selig Center estimates that California Hispanics had the highest buying power in 2006, with $214.5 billion, almost twice that of second-ranked Texas, with $140.2 billion.

The tables at right show the states with the greatest Hispanic buying power in 2006, the states with the highest shares of Hispanic buying power, and the states where Hispanic buying power grew the fastest from 1990 to 2006 (Figure 1.20).

Historically, Hispanic buying power was concentrated in a few states. However, this is changing as a growing number of states feel the impact of an increasing Hispanic population that is improving its financial well-being. Figure 1.21 shows how fast Hispanic purchasing power is growing in these areas. Note that North Carolina and Arkansas had over 1000 percent growth in the last 15 years. This decentralization is expected to continue in coming decades, creating new marketing opportunities.

Latinos as Taxpayers

Latinos, documented and undocumented, are contributing to the U.S. economy not only as consumers, but also as taxpayers, and many are not receiving the benefits of the income tax, Social Security, and Medicare programs that they are paying into. On April 5, 2005, *The New York Times* published an article by Eduardo Porter titled, "Illegal Immigrants are Bolstering Social Security with Billions," which describes how undocumented workers who use false papers to work have contributed an estimated $189 billion to the Social Security administration "earnings file" since the late 1980s. Presently, that file is growing by more than $50

FIGURE 1.19 . . . .

Ten States with Most Concentrated Hispanic Buying Power, 2006

by selected state, in percent

STATE	HISPANIC SHARE OF TOTAL BUYING POWER
New Mexico	29.6%
Texas	19.5
California	17.4
Arizona	15.2
Florida	14.6
Nevada	13.8
Colorado	11.1
New York	9.2
New Jersey	8.8
Illinois	8.3

Source: Selig Center for Economic Growth. Terry College of Business, The University of Georgia. July 2006

FIGURE 1.20 . . . .

Ten States with Highest Percentage Change in Hispanic Buying Power, 1990–2006

STATE	% CHANGE IN BUYING POWER
North Carolina	1,042%
Arkansas	1,174
Tennessee	833
Georgia	832
Nevada	748
Alabama	679
South Dakota	652
Minnesota	633
South Carolina	626
North Dakota	623

Source: Selig Center for Economic Growth. Terry College of Business, The University of Georgia. July 2006

billion a year, generating $6 to $7 billion in Social Security tax revenue and about $1.5 billion in Medicare taxes.

In other words, Latino immigration is a godsend for the U.S. economy in many ways. Hopefully, progress will be made in the near future toward a solution to clarify the status of currently undocumented immigrant workers with the creation of an efficient government program that gives immigrants the opportunity to not only contribute to society, but to get recognition and benefits for the Social Security and other taxes they pay.

In summary, present Hispanic buying power growth stems from more than the natural population increase and immigration growth. The Selig Center study states that several factors support the substantial and continued growth of Hispanic buying power. Better employment opportunities are most important, enhanced by the largest number ever of young Hispanics pursuing higher education. These young workers are entering the highly competitive workforce better prepared than ever before. This results in higher salaries and more families with higher incomes.

With this much population growth and buying power at stake, corporations need to better understand and manage the new consumer market segments that are appearing among Latinos, discussed in more detail in later chapters.

Diversity within the Market

Somebody once said, "The U.S. as a nation is like the United Nations—every country in the world is represented!" Similarly, Latinos from every Spanish-speaking country can be found in the United States; from the smallest (Uruguay, Costa Rica, Panama) to the largest (Mexico, Spain, Argentina).

It is true that the Hispanic market is not monolithic but polycultural; however, it is always necessary to keep in mind that Mexicans and people of Mexican descent represent the vast majority (63.9 percent) of the U.S. Hispanic market today.

FIGURE 1.21 ....

Hispanic Origin by Specific Country, 2005

COUNTRY	NUMBER	% OF TOTAL HISPANIC POPULATION
Mexican	26,784,268	63.9%
Caribbean	6,392,617	15.3
Puerto Rican (Continental)	3,794,268	9.1
Cuban	1,462,593	3.5
Dominican	1,135,756	2.7
Central American (non-Mexican)	3,114,877	7.2
Costa Rican	111,978	0.3
Guatemalan	780,191	1.9
Honduran	466,843	1.1
Nicaraguan	275,126	0.7
Panamanian	141,286	0.3
Salvadoran	1,240,031	3.0
Other Central American	99,422	0.2
South American	2,237,960	5.4
Argentinean	189,303	0.5
Bolivian	68,649	0.2
Chilean	105,141	0.3
Colombian	723,596	1.7
Ecuadorian	432,068	1.0
Peruvian	415,352	1.0
Uruguayan	51,646	0.1
Venezuelan	162,762	0.4
Other South American	89,443	0.2
Spanish	362,424	0.9
All Other Spanish / Hispanic / Latino	3,033,648	7.3
Total	41,926,302	100.0%

Note: Does not include the estimated 1.5 million Census undercount and 3.9 million Puerto Rican islanders.

Source: Pew Hispanic Center, tabulations of 2005 American Community Survey. "Hispanics at Mid-Decade."

Hispanic Dispersion

Latinos are responsible for much of the population growth between 1990 and 2005 in seven states: California, Texas, Florida, Arizona, Illinois, New York, and New Jersey, and represent one-third or more of the total growth in Georgia, North Carolina, Washington, Massachusetts, Colorado, and Nevada.

Despite the decentralization the Hispanic population has experienced in the past decade, Mexicans and Central Americans continue to be more concentrated in the West, Cubans in the South, and Puerto Ricans in the Northeast.

FIGURE 1.22 ·

Population by U.S. Region and Hispanic Origin, 2004

numbers in thousands

| | NORTHEAST | | MIDWEST | | SOUTH | | WEST | | TOTAL |
	#	%	#	%	#	%	#	%	*(100%)*
Mexico	593	2.2%	2,713	10.2%	9,577	36.0%	13,746	51.6%	26,630
Puerto Rico	2,309	60.1	314	8.2	917	23.9	299	7.8	3,840
Cuba	149	9.2	38	2.3	1,271	78.8	157	9.7	1,614
Non-Mexican Central America	579	18.3	139	4.4	1,165	36.9	1,274	40.4	3,158
South America	768	36.3	123	5.8	853	40.4	369	17.5	2,114
Other Hispanic	1,096	35.7	189	6.2	633	20.6	1,151	37.5	3,069
Total	5,495	13.6	3,517	8.7	14,417	35.7	16,996	42.0	40,425

Source: U.S. Census, "Population by Region, Sex, and Hispanic Origin Type, with Percent Distributions by Region, 2004."

Many Latinos move within the U.S. to follow employment opportunities. From 2004 to 2005, the number of Hispanics that relocated within the U.S. to look for a new job, or because of a lost job, was close to four times the number of white non-Hispanics who moved for similar reasons (Figure 1.23 below).

FIGURE 1.23 ·

Work Related Reasons for Moving among Hispanic and White Non-Hispanic, 2004–2005

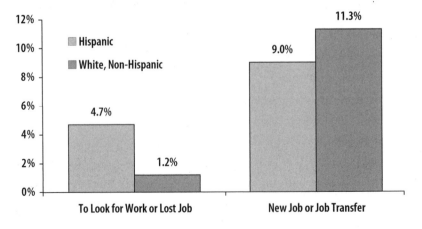

Source: M. Isabel Valdés, adapted from U.S. Census Bureau, 2005

Urban Growth

Hispanic populations historically have been concentrated in large cities. However, over the past couple of decades they have begun to move into smaller
cities. According to economist Alejandro Neut in the December 2006 issue of
Monitor Hispano, "Over the last decade, small cites (defined as having less than
50 thousand people) have experienced more growth in Hispanic population
than any other type of city. While total population in small cities grew by less
than 20 percent since 2000, the Hispanic population grew by more than 100
percent in such areas. And this is a cross country phenomenon, with Hispanic
population in small cities growing by 229 percent in the South, 191 percent in
the West, 128 percent in the Northeast, and 102 percent in the Midwest."

Hispanic population growth is noticeable at the state level across the country. As shown in Figure 1.24 below, the Hispanic population is contributing to
the growth in many states, ranging from 48 percent in North Carolina to just
under 9 percent in New York.

FIGURE 1.24 . . . .

Ten States with the Largest Increases in Hispanic Population, 2000–2005

State	Population Increase	Population Increase (percent)
California	1,792,917	16.7%
Texas	1,351,795	20.7
Florida	809,568	30.9
Arizona	411,339	32.4
Illinois	298,145	19.7
New York	243,782	8.8
New Jersey	214,117	19.5
Georgia	200,077	47.0
North Carolina	177,080	48.2
Colorado	175,200	24.5

Source: Pew Hispanic Center, tabulations of 2005 American Community Survey, "Hispanics at Mid-decade."

Nativity, Citizenship, and Undocumented Immigration

The vast majority of the U.S. Hispanic market consists of legal U.S. citizens and
legal non-citizen residents. There were 16.9 million Hispanics eligible to vote in

2005 (that is, U.S. citizens 18 and over),[9] and according to the U.S. Government an additional eight million green card holders (legal permanent residents) are eligible to become citizens, the majority of whom are of Latin American origin. Presently, there is an on-going Hispanic media and grassroots community effort ("Ya es Hora") to entice green card holders to become U.S. citizens.[10] This drive has been highly successful, as the number of citizenship applications filed has more than doubled in the previous year in Los Angeles alone. Between two and three million new Hispanic citizens are expected to be eligible to vote in the 2008 presidential elections.

The vast majority of persons of Mexican origin were either born in the U.S. (60.6 percent) or are naturalized citizens (8.5 percent). See Figure 1.25 below.

Undocumented immigration accounts for an estimated 10.7 to 11.5 million people at the present time, according to the Pew Hispanic Center. Of those, close to half (about 5 million) are estimated to be of Mexican origin. Contrary to popular belief, most of these immigrants don't cross the U.S.- Mexico border illegally. They arrive with legal documents and overstay their visas.

FIGURE 1.25 ....

Latino Immigrants by Country of Origin and Citizenship Status, 2004

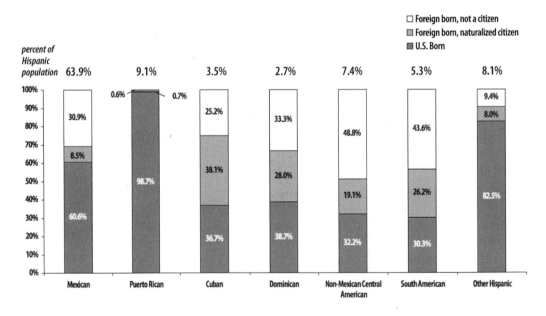

Notes: Data based on sample limited to the household population and exclude the population living in institutions, college dormitories, and other group quarters. For information on confidentiality protection, sampling error, nonsampling error, and definitions, see http://factfinder.census.gov/home/en/datanotes/exp_acs2004.html. Some percentages do not sum to 100.0 due to rounding.

Source: U.S. Census Bureau. 2004 American Community Survey. Selected Population Profiles, S0201.

Many individuals are unaware that the island of Puerto Rico is a common-wealth of the United States, and as such, all Puerto Ricans are United States citizens—those who reside in the continental U.S. (3.8 million), as well as those who live on the island (3.9 million).

FIGURE 1.26

Nativity and Citizenship Status, 2004

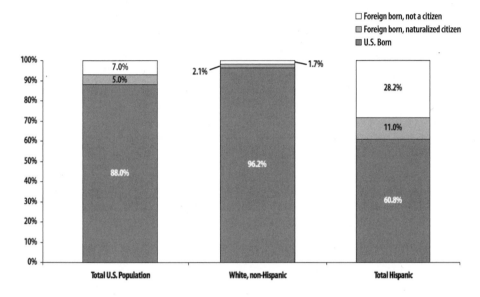

Notes: Total Hispanic column includes Puerto Rico. Data based on sample limited to the household population and exclude the population living in institutions, college dormitories, and other group quarters. Data does not take into account the estimated Census undercount. For information on confidentiality protection, sampling error, nonsampling error, and definitions, see http://factfinder.census.gov/home/en/datanotes/exp_acs2004.html. Some percentages do not sum to 100.0 due to rounding.

Source: U.S. Census Bureau. 2004 American Community Survey. Selected Population Profiles, S0201.

Resulting from the large immigration waves of the past several decades, foreign-born, non-U.S. citizens are most likely Hispanic (see Figure 1.26), hence the focus on Hispanics in particular when immigration is discussed.

Targeting Hispanics: Country of Origin Makes a Difference

U.S. Hispanics come from every Spanish-speaking country in the world, but the majority (63.9 percent) are from Mexico or of Mexican descent, followed at a distance by Central American and South American countries (Figures 1.25 and 1.27).

FIGURE 1.27 . . . .

Population by Hispanic Origin, 2004

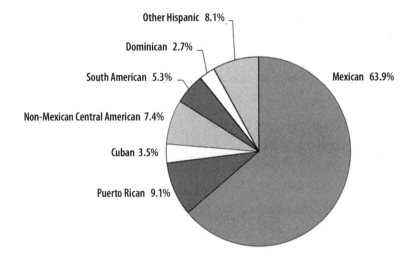

Source: M. Isabel Valdés, Pew Hispanics at Mid-Decade 2005, population by region, sex, and Hispanic origin type, based on U.S. Census.

Due to the higher concentration of Caribbean Latinos, Mexicans, and Central and South Americans in some regions, and the growing geographic dispersion taking place, (see the previous section, *Hispanic Dispersion*), it is valuable for marketers to identify where sub-segments concentrate geographically and what is unique to each sub-culture. For example, Mexicans are not only the largest Hispanic consumer sub-group, but they also have the largest share of Latino youth (consumers under age 20), 39.5 percent. In comparison, Cubans are the oldest group; 25 percent of Hispanics of Cuban origin or descent are under age 20, while 21 percent are aged 65 and older (compared to 4 percent of Mexicans).[11] (See Figure 1.21 in the *Diversity within the Market* section earlier in this chapter for more details.)

Presently, with the help of computer technology, it is easy to determine the concentration of Hispanic immigrants by country of origin down to the zip-code level. This is especially useful for retailers, banks, churches, and local governments that would benefit by developing an *in-culture*—or culturally attuned—local Hispanic communication strategy for merchandising and advertising. This is also useful when micro-targeting consumers with a specific country of origin through direct mail and telemarketing campaigns.

Geo-segmentation can facilitate finding zip codes with high concentrations of Cubans, Puerto Ricans, Dominicans, and Caribbean Latinos versus high concentrations of Mexicans and Central Americans. The marketer can then adapt the message, media mix, and visuals of direct-mail pieces to target the specific sub-group that is predominant in each zip code. Note also that to Spanish-speakers, accents are distinctive. Thus, a television advertisement in Miami targeted to a Cuban audience, but using a Mexican Spanish accent may fall flat.

In-culture "fine tuning" to the specific country of origin's vocabulary and culture adds much emotional value in addition to helping avoid marketing "snafus." Therefore, whenever possible, take advantage of country-specific background information, such as the value of your brand, product, category, or service in the different regions where Latinos from specific countries concentrate. This will add a "culturally correct" tonality and feel to help engage the consumer, providing a safety net to the campaign, program, or service. It will also increase the chances of effective, memorable, creative ad campaigns. The safest approach to make sure these Hispanic cultural nuances are correct is to test it with target consumers in focus groups or other quantitative formats that provide a space for in-depth probing.

ATENCIÓN   REGION-SPECIFIC SEGMENTATION

REGION-SPECIFIC SEGMENTATION CAN HELP YOU:

- **Fine-tune your business plan and other financial estimates.** Some regions are significantly more active in some categories.

- **Estimate "brand heritage" or lack thereof and brand development strategy.** Many U.S. brands are marketed in some Latin American countries but not in others, hence the need for fine-tuning your marketing strategy or some elements of it depending on the dominant country of origin in the specific region.

- **Ascertain category differences.** For example, the popular cuisine from some countries includes some ingredients that are not used—or popular—in the cuisine of other Latin American countries.

- **Bullet-proof acceptability.** Make sure your national or regional target marketing efforts are culturally attuned to "talk to" your target segment, visually as well as verbally, in the specific region.

- **Use country-specific "cultural cues."** They are key to touching emotional buttons.

A new type of diversity is growing within the Hispanic market as multi-racial marriages continue to increase. The 2000 Census found about 6.8 million people who identified themselves as multi-racial. In addition, the number of black Latinos, or "Garifunas," is also becoming more visible (as described later in this chapter, Hispanic/Latino is not a race). These multi-racial families bring a novel angle to the market, and as they grow in number in the coming decades, they will present unique opportunities and challenges.

U.S. Hispanics vs. Hispanics Abroad

Hispanics in the continental United States are better off financially than most Hispanics living in Latin America. Their per capita income is higher than that in any Latin American country (Figure 1.28). Until the economies, living conditions, and opportunities improve in many Latin American countries, the U.S. will continue to be a magnet for Hispanic immigration. Hence, increased corporate manufacturing, investments, and opportunities in Latin America should be included in corporate growth plans for present and future decades.

FIGURE 1.28 . . . .

Selected Countries GDP Per Capita

Hispanic income per capita, 2005

COUNTRY	PER CAPITA INCOME ($US)
Total U.S.	$44,190
U.S. Hispanics	$20,000*
Spain	27,767
Brazil	5,717
Peru	3,374
Argentina	5,458
Chile	8,864
Mexico	8,066
Costa Rica	4,858
Uruguay	6,007
Venezuela	6,736
El Salvador	2,619
Guatemala	2,508
Honduras	1,213

Figure represents per capita income of U.S. Hispanics.

Sources: U.S. Hispanics—PEW Hispanics at Mid-Decade 2005, Other Countries—International Monetary Fund, World Economic Outlook Database, April 2007.

Hispanic or Latino?

Most foreign-born Latinos use their country of origin to refer to themselves, e.g., I am Mexican, or Puerto Rican, or El Salvadoran.

The term Latino appeared on the U.S. Census for the first time in 2000. People who marked "other Spanish/Hispanic/Latino" had additional space to specify their Hispanic origins, such as Salvadoran or Dominican, a practice started in the 1990 Census.

Presently, Hispanic consumers in some areas such as California and Texas tend to prefer Latino. When referring to a particular Hispanic group, however, the name of the country of origin is usually used.

There is currently no consensus within the Hispanic community as to how to refer to its members collectively. What do people of Hispanic origin prefer? In a Gallup poll conducted in mid-2001, Americans of Spanish origin overwhelmingly said they preferred "Hispanic" rather than "Latino," by 67 percent to 13 percent. However, regardless of which term they favor, few Hispanics say they are significantly bothered by the use of either term.

Hispanic/Latino is Not a Race

Although many people think of Hispanic or Latino as being a racial designation, it is not. People who consider themselves among the ethnic group called Hispanic or Latino can be of any race—black, white, Asian, Mestizo Indian, etc. Because Hispanics may be of any race, the Census Bureau usually refers to non-Hispanic whites—people who have said they are white, but have indicated they are not Hispanic. For marketers and advertisers, the fact to remember is that the Hispanic market is not monolithic, and that Hispanics and Latinos may represent many different racial groups.

For example, black ethnic Latinos called Garifunas are the largest black ethnic group in Central America, with vibrant communities in Honduras, Belize, Guatemala, Nicaragua, and the United States. Every spring in Los Angeles they celebrate the Annual Garifuna Day Street Festival. There are over 20,000 Garifunas living in Los Angeles alone.

ATENCIÓN   RACE

For the first time in Census 2000, respondents could chose from one of 63 options about race, including more than one race; only about 2 percent of respondents chose more than one race.

From the glossary of the 2000 census:

"Spanish/Hispanic/Latino is a self-designated classification for people whose origins are from Spain, the Spanish-speaking countries of Central or South America, the Caribbean, or those identifying themselves generally as Spanish, Spanish-American, etc. Categories listed on the U.S. Census 2000 include: Mexican, Puerto Rican, Cuban, other Spanish, Hispanic, or Latino."

In 1990, Census respondents could select their race from one of only five categories: "white," "black," "American Indian, Eskimo or Aleutian," "Asian or Pacific Islander," or "some other race."

Summary

The U.S. Hispanic market has entered a new stage; the younger U.S. born/second generation is becoming the lead generation in the marketplace. The 2000 U.S. Census data and subsequent updates from the U.S. Census, the Pew Hispanic Center, TRPI, the Selig Center, and other organizations confirmed what Hispanic-marketing experts already knew. The U.S. Hispanic market continues to contribute to the U.S. market, not only in size, but also in dramatically increasing income and business ownership. Educational attainment has improved slightly, voter participation is significantly higher and more powerful than a decade ago, and larger numbers of Hispanics are joining the middle class and learning about wealth creation.

Regionalization is still driven by country of origin. Mexicans, Cubans, Puerto Ricans and others tend to concentrate and start businesses in the states where they have historically settled. However, the shift to new areas is now evident as Hispanics can be found in every state of the Union. Moreover, they are becoming the "majority minority" in several states where a decade ago Latinos were a definite minority. With more and more Hispanics joining the middle class, more businesses have targeted Hispanics, learning to capitalize on the opportunity presented by these "instant new consumers." The year 2050 will be the "tipping point"; the U.S. Census projects that by that time, Latinos, along with other ethnic population segments, will exceed 50 percent of the U.S. population. Estimates for the Hispanic market share vary from 25 percent to 27 percent of the total population of 2050, with great opportunities and income potential.

Certainly, not all is rosy. The Hispanic community continues to face many challenges such as a growing number of teenage mothers, high school dropout rates, alcoholism and drug usage, poverty, rising suicide rates, lack of health insurance, and problems related to undocumented immigrants.

Fortunately, corporate America is increasingly supportive, addressing some of these problems in the Hispanic community while leveraging the marketing benefits of a "Share of Heart" strategy. By providing on-the-job training and greater contributions to scholarship funds, there is a definite movement in their leadership to improve education and create a healthy, wealthy, well-adapted, acculturating Hispanic American market.

Notes

1   U.S. Census Bureau. Post-Censual Population Estimate, May 2007.

2   Seoane, M. and M. M. Isabel Valdés. *The Hispanic Market Book.* Gale Research Publishers, 1995.

3   U.S. Census Bureau, Press Release, March 18, 2004.

4   Ibid.

5   Ibid.

6   Pew Hispanic Center. "Hispanics at Mid-Decade. Race and Ethnicity by Sex and Age." 2005.

7   Captura Group. "Connecting with the U.S. Hispanic Market Online." Idiom Technologies, Inc., 2006.

8   Pew Hispanic Center. Tabulations of 2005 American Community Survey.

9   Pew Hispanic Center, from U.S. Census Bureau. American Fact Finder Tables B05003 and B050031.

10   Jordan, Miriam. "Univision Gives Citizenship Drive an Unusual Lift." *The Wall Street Journal*, May 10, 2007.

11   U.S. Census Bureau. "Population by Sex, Age, and Hispanic Origin Type." 2004.

CHAPTER 2

Born/Not Born in the USA

Since my early days designing and executing qualitative and quantitative marketing research studies in the 1980s, it became evident that there are marked socio-demographic and psychographic differences between U.S. and foreign-born Latino generations. The observed differences enticed me to divide the Hispanic market into two major groups gauging the ways in which these were different—or similar—and when or how these differences or similarities were relevant to marketing and advertising.

The U.S.-born and foreign-born Hispanic generations or segments have continued to grow and mature, deepening the differences in their socio-demographic and psychographic characteristics. Compared with the previous decades, the foreign-born segment was so significantly larger than the second or third generations that only occasionally was it relevant to target these more acculturated Latinos. This has changed dramatically from those earlier days. The current size and exponential growth of these two generational segments have direct implications for business, marketing and communications, not only because they are significant in size, but also because they are more often than not culturally different—requiring distinct insights, marketing and communications strategies. What is referred to as "generational distance" impacts the socio-cultural dynamics of U.S.-born Latinos, as does length of residence and age upon arrival in the United States.

As a matter of fact, the Hispanic market today is undergoing a massive psycho-social and cultural shift due to the fact that the U.S.-born generations are rapidly surpassing both in size and relevance in the marketplace the foreign-born segments and further fragmenting the Hispanic market. In other words, the generational crossover has arrived!

This chapter looks in depth at the socio-demographic differences of the U.S.-born and foreign-born generations. Paying attention to the generational shifts and differences can be the difference between a minor marketing accomplishment and a huge marketing triumph

Presently it is becoming a more popular practice in Hispanic marketing, advertising, and communications to target these segments separately—or in combination—the different sub-segments of each generation. Therefore there is growing value in having the statistics for both generations and sub-generations readily available. This section reviews in detail basic statistics and data useful for developing, analyzing, and writing marketing strategies for these sub-segments and throughout this book, when distinctions between generations are called for, they are included in the analysis.

The Hispanic market will continue its growth curve mostly through new births as well as new immigration. Both segments present valuable business opportunities. On the one hand, the vast majority of the foreign-born (G1) immigrants are adults upon arrival and therefore become instant potential consumers that may be of value to your business category. On the other, the continued growth of the U.S.-born generational segments—(G2, G3+)—will require a growing body of knowledge and insights as the cultural diversity and socio-demographic differences within the market deepen. The aim of this chapter is to provide simple and practical tools to successfully manage this growing and profitable market.

FIGURE 2.1 . . . .

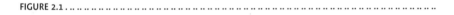

Hispanic Population by U.S.-Born and Foreign-Born Generations, 2006

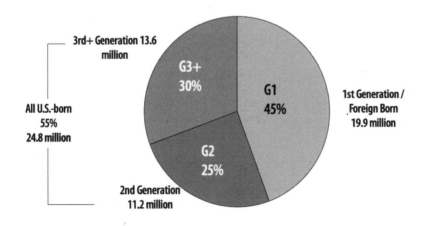

Source: M. Isabel Valdés, 2007. The 2006 data is consistent with independent estimates including those from the Pew Hispanic Center and the Census Bureau's 2006 March Current Population Survey, Annual Social and Economic Supplement.

Foreign Born: G1

Foreign-born, first-generation immigrants represent a 20 million-consumer segment (or 21.5 million after adding the 1.5 million estimated Latino population undercount from the last census). They constitute 45 percent of the Hispanic market.

Demographic differences that can impact business strategy are evident between U.S.-born and foreign-born segments. For example, U.S.-born Latinos are significantly younger than their foreign-born counterparts, as the majority are children of the waves of Latino immigrants that occurred during the past three decades (see Latino Generational Cross-Over, Chapter 1, Figure 1.3).

The population of foreign-born Hispanics will continue to grow both from new immigration in response to labor market needs and also as U.S.-citizen Latinos continue to bring their children and family members to join them.

FIGURE 2.2

Fertility in the Past Year by Hispanic Generation, by Race and Ethnicity, 2005

women with a birth in past year, 2005 household population defined for women aged 15 to 44 years ,

	ALL	PERCENT	SHARE OF ALL U.S. WOMEN
All Hispanic	**900,729**	**9.2**	**21.3**
US Born; 2nd ,3rd+ Generations	397,133	7.9	9.4
Foreign Born / 1st Generation	503,596	10.5	11.9
White, not Hispanic	2,397,341	6.3	56.8
Black, not Hispanic	603,047	7.4	14.3
Asian, not Hispanic	214,882	7.0	5.1
Other, not Hispanic	106,081	6.8	2.5
Total	4,222,080	7.0	100.0

Source: M. Isabel Valdés, adapted from Pew Hispanic Center. Tabulations of 2005 American Community Survey.

Born in the USA: G2, G3+

The U.S.-born or "native" Hispanic market segment includes the second (G2), third (G3) and prior generations of Hispanics that have resided in the U.S. for anywhere from a few years to over 500 years. Prior generations of Hispanics were composed almost entirely of persons of Mexican or Spanish descent. U.S-born Hispanics are close to 25 million strong and represent 55 percent of the domestic Latino population today. Add the 3.9 million Puerto Rican Islanders—also American citizens—and the "true size" of the U.S.-born Hispanic market segment is 29 million.

The growth rate of the U.S.-born (G2 and G3+) Hispanic segment will continue to accelerate for several reasons, even in a hypothetical "zero" Hispanic migration scenario. First, Latinos are young and tend to have more children than the average non-Hispanic family. Second, many of the offspring of the large wave of foreign-born Latinos of the last three decades are now in their childbearing ages, contributing disproportionately to the dramatic growth of new Hispanic citizens. Even though more-acculturated Hispanics tend to have smaller families and there is also a slow-growing trend for U.S. Latinos to have fewer children than their foreign-born counterparts, Latino average household sizes continue to be larger than the general market. Lastly, as previously stated, the Latino population is younger overall; hence their death rate is presently lower than the general population's, and the greater number of births over deaths in this population contributes to the fast overall population growth.

Because acculturation and life experience can vary drastically between U.S.-born generations (G2 and G3+), it is necessary to make the distinction between these generations for marketing and communications purposes. For an in-depth analysis of generational differences, see the GenAge segmentation in Chapter 7, which presents the "U.S.-born" segment data divided by generations and shows the considerable marketing implications of acculturation and immigration-based differences in key age groups.

FIGURE 2.3 . . . .

Parentage of U.S.-Born Second Generation Hispanics, aged 25 to 54 Years, March 2005

Mixed Parentage (one parent foreign-born, one parent U.S.-born)	41.4%
Foreign parentage (both parents foreign-born)	22.8%

Source: *Monthly Labor Review.* "Labor Force Characteristics of Second-Generation Americans." September 2006.

The Generational and Cultural Cross-Over

Latinos born in the U.S. can be grouped into two distinct marketing "platforms" or "plateaus":

- First, the "young millennial Latinos"—children, teens, and young adults born to foreign-born parents (G2)

- Second, "traditional Latinos"—those born to Latino families that have been U.S. citizens for two or more generations (G3+)

FIGURE 2.4 . . . .

Median Age by Generation, Foreign-Born and U.S.-Born Latinos,
race and gender 2005

	TOTAL	MALE	FEMALE
Hispanic	27	26	27
U.S. Born (G2, G3+)	17	16	18
Foreign Born (G1)	35	34	36
White *	40	39	41
Black *	31	29	33
Asian *	35	34	35
Other*	24	22	25
Total	36	35	37

*Non-Hispanic

Source: Pew Hispanic Center. Tabulations of 2005 American Community Survey.

G2: Latino Millennials

The first group, the "millennial Latinos," has become more visible in the marketplace during the past decade. They are the vanguard of what is to come in the Hispanic marketplace in the next two decades. Young adults G2s lead the growing cultural cross-over as they are more acculturated than previous generation of Latinos, re-shaping their identity and what is to be Hispanic today. Many more Latinos in the G2 generation have acculturated faster than prior generations. Several factors seem to speed up the acculturation process including the degree of urbanity of their area of residence, (for example large city versus small city), the size and concentration of the Hispanic population in the area or "critical mass," (the more concentrated the Hispanic population, the slower the acculturation patterns), the educational attainment of the parents, and last, the personality of the individual; some people adapt faster than others. Also, it is possible that greater access to general market media and education have also contributed to the faster acculturation process. Jennifer Lopez is an example of this new generation of American Latinos. They know how to live in both cultures and enjoy doing so.

Presently most G2s concentrate in the younger age groups (84 % are under age fourteen); 95 percent of all the infants age 0 to 5 in the Hispanic market today, 87 percent of those aged 6 to 9, and 84 percent of the children aged 10 to 14 (see Figure 2.5).

FIGURE 2.5 . . . .

Young Millennial (G2) Latinos, 2005

AGES	U.S. BORN	FOREIGN BORN
0–5	95%	5%
6–9	87	13
10–14	84	16

Source: M. Isabel Valdés, GenAge segmentation 2006

The majority of these children are growing up in a different world and acculturation phase than their parents. They are children of first generation immigrants, living in a world with many more opportunities, which is more open to Latinos than it was to their parents; however, they have to deal with their parents' cultural "gaps," contradictions and conflicts—such as immigration—as well as with more cultural adaptation issues.

G3+: The "Traditional" Hispanic Market

The youngsters born to deeply rooted, multiple-generation Latino families tend to present different socio-psychographic profiles. Most are significantly acculturated into mainstream American culture, speak English fluently, as would be expected. However, depending on the market, the levels of value-orientation and acculturation levels may vary drastically. For example, G3+ Latinos who live in Phoenix, Arizona, San Jose, California, or San Antonio, Texas may not always speak Spanish fluently and be active and successful in American society and businesses. However, they may be fond of Hispanic traditional values and highly family-centered. They may have adopted some of the American cultural values and orientation, but their identity as Hispanics can be much more traditional and stronger than expected. Other, larger urban market G3's may have moved one-hundred percent away from traditional Hispanic cultural values, and feel perfectly comfortable being independent and not family centered. More of the latter can be found in New York, Chicago, and San Francisco and the factors that contribute to this faster acculturation process tend to be the same as those mentioned in the case of G2's acculturation.

The relevant point here is to be aware that these differences exist and to know how to identify which of these presents the best business opportunity for you.

Depending on your product or service category, it is recommended that you ascertain where your "sweet spot" target audience falls in the acculturation continuum. Is your "sweet spot" composed of a mix? Is it the first generation (G1) with several decades of residence in the U.S., plus the young U.S. born adults (G2 and G3+)? Then, select the in-culture marketing strategy that is commensurate with your target. This subject is developed further in the GenAge segmentation section (Chapter 7).

Income: U.S. Born vs. Foreign Born

Hispanic household income analysis by generation reveals differences between segments. On average, U.S.-born households have higher incomes than foreign-born households (see Chapter 1, Hispanic Purchasing Power section).

FIGURE 2.6 . . . .

Hispanic Median Household Income by U.S.-Born/Foreign-Born Generations, 2005

	MEDIAN INCOME
Total Hispanic	$36,000
U.S.-born Hispanic (2nd Generation, 3rd Generation and Greater)	$39,000
Foreign-born Hispanic (1st generation)	$34,000
Total U.S.	$45,200

Source: Adapted from "Hispanics at Mid-Decade" and Pew Hispanic Center, tabulations of 2005 American Community Survey.

U.S.-born income analysis by age shows comparable incomes between the second and third generations, except for in the 55 and older age group, where second generation Hispanics have a considerably larger income.

FIGURE 2.7 . . . .

Median Annual Individual Earnings of U.S.-Born Hispanics
by generation and age, 2004

	SECOND GENERATION	THIRD GENERATION
Total U.S.-born Hispanics	$30,069	$30,500
16 to 24 years	$18,720	$19,967
25 to 54 years	$33,292	$32,694
55 years and older	$39,210	$30,667

Source: "Labor Force Characteristics of Second-Generation Americans." *Monthly Labor Review.* September 2006.

Multi-Generational, Multi-Cultural Households

Multi-generational households are common in the U.S. Hispanic marketplace, and there may be generational differences within the household. Parents may be bi-lingual, Spanish-preferred; the grandparents and uncles mono-lingual Spanish; and the children bi-lingual English preferred.

These family households often experience "acculturation stress" in action. Foreign-born Latino parents who acquired their culture, values, and behaviors from their countries of origin will often have values and behaviors quite different from those of their acculturating children. These children and teens raised in the United States usually acquire at least some of their values and preferences from their peers in school, the media, friends, and so forth. For these reasons, even within households, Hispanic families can frequently exhibit distinct sets of aspirations, behaviors, food preferences, cooking styles, and media consumption habits.

FIGURE 2.8 . . . .

Multi-generational Households

by country of origin and generation, 1998–2002

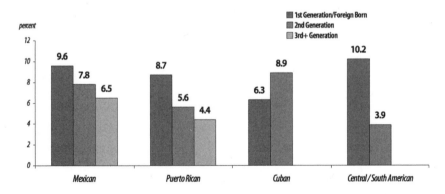

Source: N. Landale et. Al. 2006. Chapter 4 in *Hispanics and the Future of America* in Marta Tienda, 2007.

For example, an Anglo-American DJ was asked about his experience deejaying for a Quinceañera: "Usually when I DJ for kids, they want to hear the same 20 or 30 modern popular songs. Here it was much different. Some kids wanted hip-hop—American youth music—but others wanted Salsa, Meringue,

Duranguese, and Reggaeton." This DJ was seeing children raised with different levels of acculturation; some wanted to hear the music that U.S. teens listen to, whereas others wanted to hear Hispanic music, and even those teens were further subdivided as to the sort of music they preferred to hear, reflecting their varied Hispanic backgrounds!

Hispanic household data shows the majority of the children reside with a parent head of household. However, among foreign-born children, fewer live with one of their parents as head of the household and more have other living arrangements, such as living with an aunt, uncle, sibling, or another member of their extended family. Significantly fewer live with a grandparent head of household than U.S.-born children. (Figure 2.9). This may be the result of immigrants who come to the U.S. as young adults and are often the first in their families to immigrate, while their spouses, parents, and siblings still live in their country of origin. Those who immigrated, however, may share housing with other young Latinos or find temporary living arrangements with extended family or friends.

FIGURE 2.9 . . . .

Living Arrangements of Children, 2005

	PARENT HOUSEHOLDER	GRANDPARENT HOUSEHOLDER	OTHER*
Hispanic	**85.3%**	**7.3%**	**7.4%**
U.S. Born; 2nd/3rd + Generations	85.8	7.8	6.4
Foreign Born	81.5	3.2	15.4
Total U.S. Population	88.8	6.4	4.8

*Other relatives (siblings, aunts, uncles, cousins), friends of the family, etc.

Source: M. Isabel Valdés, based on Pew Hispanic Center tabulations of 2005 American Community Survey.

Figure 2.9 shows that, with the exception of Cuban households, a considerable number of foreign-born families have multi-generational households.

In sum, the traditional "foreign-born" and "U.S. born" Latino market segments continue to be highly relevant when selecting the "sweet spot, " or high value segments. However, these have shifted demographically; the U.S. born Latinos to foreign-born parents present a quite different psychographic profile than those born to "deep rooted" Hispanic parents, with more than three generations in the United States. The foreign-born Hispanic population segment has also changed significantly; a large percentage are joining the baby-boomers, and while new immigrants continue to arrive in the U.S., their numbers are significantly smaller than in the 1970s through the 1990s. The latter are new consumers that need to be introduced to the marketplace, brands, and categories, whereas the previous waves of U.S. born have moved along the acculturation continuum, at a different pace and have acquired English language and other skills, and also many have become American citizens and active members in American society.

The acculturating Hispanic market can be challenging to manage and target successfully. Hence, I have developed a couple of new marketing tools, with visuals and demographic data that should facilitate successful business development and marketing to Latinos in the next decade.

CHAPTER 3

Recovering the Latino Soul

The In-Culture Approach is a 360-degree "holistic" marketing strategy that incorporates not only consumer behavior but also every aspect of culture and history that directly or indirectly, consciously or unconsciously, has an impact on the cultural and value orientation (mind-set, traits, dreams, fears, and lifestyle) of the consumers' decision-making process. Hence there is need to briefly contextualize the Hispanic market's "Weltanschauung," both its past and historical perspective, as well as some of the pressing social issues taking place today.

In addition, historic background information provides a rich base of material that bright, creative minds can use in the development of In-Culture communications strategies.

Few people are aware of the surprising scope of contributions Hispanics have made throughout U.S. history. The history of the Hispanic presence in the United States dates back five centuries to 1513, before Jamestown, the first permanent British colony, was established in Virginia in 1607. St. Augustine, Florida, founded in 1565 by the Spanish admiral Pedro Menendez de Aviles, served as Spain's military headquarters in North America for the rest of the 16th century, and remains to this day the oldest city on the North American continent.[1] By 1790, Spain controlled a large part of what is now the United States. Many Mexican families settled in what became Texas and California long before these territories were incorporated into the Union. These Mexicans and Spaniards built roads and urbanized the West, making possible the fast advance and "conquest of the West" by General Custer. I've often heard it said that these early Hispanics never migrated, but rather, "the border migrated over their heads." The number of Hispanic immigrants has swelled since World War II. Many were brought in by state governments to provide a labor force during the war. This was the main reason for Mexican migration to Chicago prior to 1945.

Surveys identify the various motives for relocating to the United States.

Of these, economic considerations rate highest among Mexicans, whereas avoidance of political strife dominates among Cuban immigrants.[2] Family reunification, educational opportunities, new sources of financial investment, and the desire to start a new business in the United States were also identified as important contributors to Hispanic immigration.

FIGURE 3.1 . .

Territory Acquired by the U.S. in 1848 (The Treaty of Guadalupe Hidalgo) at the end of the Mexican-American War (1845–1848)

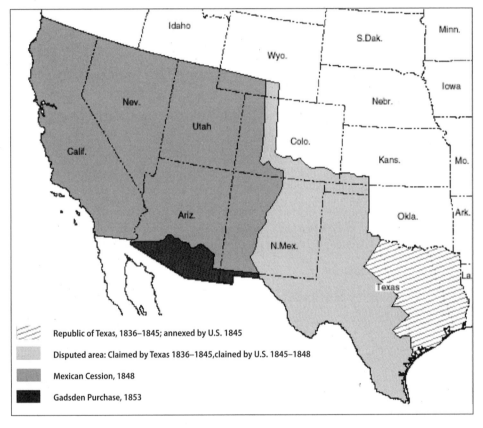

Republic of Texas, 1836–1845; annexed by U.S. 1845

Disputed area: Claimed by Texas 1836–1845,clained by U.S. 1845–1848

Mexican Cession, 1848

Gadsden Purchase, 1853

Source: www.historicaldocuments.com

The experience of immigration is a mixed bag, and is as varied as the immigrant population. Immigrant stories are often amazing—and sometimes terrifying—stories of desperate searches for better quality of life for self and family. A growing number of books recount these diverse stories; *Enrique's Journey,* by Sonia Nazario, is the story of one boy's odyssey to reunite with his mother (Random House, 2006); Julia Alvarez reveals her personal memoirs of growing up Hispanic American in *How the Garcia Girls Lost Their Accents* (Plume Publishing, 1992); *Strangers Among Us: Latino Lives in a Changing America*, by Roberto Suro, reveals rich observations of immigrants' lives (Vintage, 1999); *The Cuban American Experience: Issues, Perceptions, and Realities*, by Guarione Diaz, depicts a vibrant community with a distinct cultural identity (Reedy Press, 2007); Paul Cuadros describes the history of Latinos in the South in *A Home on the Field* (Rayo, 2006); David Hayes-Bautista's latest book, *La Nueva California, Latinos in the Golden State*, (University of California Press, 2004) addresses the positive force Latinos, and specifically Mexican Americans, have played and will continue to play in the growth of California.

In addition, there has been an increase in published works detailing the many significant contributions made by Latinos in the past. For example, Dr. Hayes-Bautista brought to the public's attention the work of Reginaldo Francisco del Valle, a Latino who participated in the foundation of the University of California at Los Angeles. Another example is the Oral History Project, dedicated to gathering and disseminating information about U.S. Latinos who participated in World War II through videotaped interviews of over 500 Hispanic soldiers and family members.

Many efforts like these are being made throughout the U.S. to recover links to Latino history and contributions, helping solidify the place U.S. Latinos have earned in American society and, in so doing, create a new positive image of these of unsung heroes.

Language is a central component of Latino soul and culture, yet only recently has it begun to be recognized and appreciated as a valuable asset in a global economy. Many non-Latino families are encouraging their children to learn Spanish as well as Chinese and Japanese, and the number of commercially available Spanish language books, films, CDs, and plays has grown exponentially in the past decade.

"Latinidad": The Identity Issue

A definition for the sake of clarity! According to Federico Subervi and Diana Rios, whose article, "Latino Identity & Situational Latinidad, appeared in *Hispanic Marketing and Public Relations*:

> "Latino identity or 'identidad Latina' is both a simple concept as well as a complex one. At the most basic level, it is a state of mind that propels

a person to state: "I am Latino" or "I am Latina" simply because he or she considers him or herself Latino or Latina. There may be one or many reasons for such a sense of identification, which can be expressed internally (to self) or externally (to others). In essence, that identity is a personal declaration of being part of a group called Latino.

"Furthermore, Latino identity is also an existence defined, established, guided, or pressured by self (and others, such as), family, neighborhood (media), and society. It is most complex when specifics are taken into consideration regarding which internal and/or external factors are most important for the societal-level recognition of that identity, and also how, where, and with whom that identity is expressed."[3]

What makes a person a Latino has become a subject of much interest to the Hispanic marketing and advertising trade in the recent past as well as to the academic world, including sociologists, psychologists, communications specialists, philosophers, and others who have studied this subject for decades. A short list of books recently published that address Hispanic identity include: *Hispanic/Latino Identity: A Philosophical Perspective*, by Jorge J. E. Gracia (Blackwell Publishers, 2000); *Brown: The Last Discovery of America*, by Richard Rodriguez (Viking Adult, 2002); *Hispanic Nation: Culture, Politics and the Constructing of Identity*, by Geoffrey E. Fox (The University of Arizona Press, 1996); and *Latino Cultural Citizenship: Claiming Identity, Space, and Rights*, William V. Flores and Rina Benmayor, editors (Beacon Press, 1998). In addition, hundreds of peer-reviewed research papers have been published, many in *The Hispanic Research Journal*. (Amazon.com carries all or most of these.)

Most of the academic works tend to be more theoretical or philosophical in nature, and sometimes hard to apply to the marketing and advertising world. To fill in this gap, the Association of Hispanic Advertising Agencies (AHAA), under the direction of its then-chairman Carl Kravetz, conducted a comprehensive and complete study, the Latino Identity Project, that developed a "new model" for the Hispanic advertising trade. It incorporates in its analysis and hypothesis the findings of many of the books, papers and data from the perspective—and experience—of advertising practitioners. The Latino Identity Project report concluded that what makes Latinos is their "interconnectedness . . . [that] it is not confined to [their] language and acculturation. . . . These do have a role, but only a supportive one. . . . At the center of the new model is a Heart and a set of contextual factors that interact with and continuously reshape the Heart."[4]

From the consumer standpoint, many Latinos face "identity conflicts" today—a lack of clarity about who they are, what their roots and history are, whether they "belong" and are as much U.S. citizens as any U.S. citizen. This is the natural result of the process and experiences of being raised in two cultures. Research we conducted during the past three decades showed a tendency towards a negative self-image and identity, particularly among Latino youth. This has changed dramatically and many today are very proud of being Latino, enjoying showing their "Latinidad"—and this trend still seems to be going strong. Needless to say, there is still a long way to go until Latino's identity issues become history. As mentioned in the first chapter of this book, there is a strong movement to "fully recover the Latino soul." Hispanic generations to come will benefit from the road being paved today, not only with greater participation in business and politics, but also in the areas of art, literature, and history that will most likely reduce the identity crisis and the lack of respect and recognition many Latinos experience today. Then we will all benefit from "the best of both worlds."

The Immigrant Experience

It is a challenging, and many times painful process to migrate. It is a loss on many levels. Marketers aware of this fact can leverage this and not only help alleviate the loss by making consumers feel welcomed and "a part of the American family," but also recognize the value of nostalgia in Hispanic strategies directed at the foreign-born segment. According to Celia Falicov's article, "Ambiguous Loss: Risk and Resilience in Latino Immigrant Families," which appeared in *Latinos: Remaking America*:

> "Latino immigrants, like many other immigrants, experience some degree of loss, grief, and mourning. The experiences have been compared with the processes of grief and mourning precipitated by the death of loved ones (Shuval 1982; Warheit et al. 1985; Grinberg and Grinberg 1989; Volkan and Zintl 1993). Here I will argue, however, that migration loss has special characteristics that distinguish it from other kinds of losses. Compared with the clear-cut, inescapable fact of death, migration loss is both larger and smaller. It is larger because migration brings with it losses of all kinds. Gone are family and friends who stay behind, gone is the native language, the customs and rituals, and gone is the land itself. The

ripples of these losses touch the extended kin back home and reach into the future generations born in the new land.

"Yet migration loss is also smaller than death, because despite the grief and mourning occasioned by physical, cultural, and social separation, the losses are not absolutely clear, complete, and irretrievable. Everything is still alive but is just not immediately reachable or present. Unlike the finality of death, after migration it is always possible to fantasize the eventual return or a forthcoming reunion. Furthermore, immigrants seldom migrate toward a social vacuum. A relative, friend, or acquaintance usually waits on the other side to help with work and housing and to provide guidelines for the new life. A social community and ethnic neighborhood reproduce in pockets of remembrance, the sights, sounds, smells, and tastes of one's country. All of these elements create a mix of emotions—sadness and elation, loss and restitution, absence and presence—that makes grieving incomplete, postponed, ambiguous."[5]

The "stressors" that Latinos and other immigrants experience working toward adapting and succeeding in their new country are fertile grounds to uncover rich emotional material to market and advertise in-culture, particularly when the strategy is positive and light, touching the heart.

Immigration is as American as Apple Pie

To understand the Hispanic market today, we cannot escape the Latino immigration debate, its roots, and history. With the obvious exception of Native Americans, all American citizens today trace their roots to immigrants.

A brief review of U.S. history proves that the United States owes its rapid population growth, as well as, in large part, its technological and economic success to immigrants from all over the world and their many contributions over the past few centuries.

The rationale for most immigrants to relocate to a new country continues to be the same as it was 200 years ago: to find better living conditions or business opportunities, to escape religious or political persecution, and/or to join family members. The ongoing immigration phenomenon we see today is the history of the United States.

From highly skilled professionals, to semi-skilled and unskilled workers nationwide, today's (and most probably tomorrow's) U.S. economy will continue to absorb foreign-born labor (see *Latinos in the Labor Force* in Chapter 4).

Obtaining a more in-depth understanding of Latino history can only enrich and help your marketing efforts.

The Immigration "Blind Spot"

It is a shortsighted blind spot to perceive Latino immigration as a "burden to society." In fact, today Latino labor sustains many service industries and if Latinos were not available, the lack would seriously imperil several business sectors. Latino labor also is a source of hope for anticipated future workforce shortages. A recent article in the Los Angeles Times addressed this blind spot:

> "As many in Congress, in the media and in homes across the country debate the best way to stem the flow of undocumented workers across the Rio Grande, they don't seem to be aware that this perceived problem is becoming increasingly irrelevant. In fact, the immigration concern of the future could well be how to entice Mexicans and other Latin Americans to cross into the U.S. in the numbers we need.

> ". . . the U.S. is on the brink of its massive demographic change. The first baby boomers are becoming eligible for Social Security benefits, and over the next 25 years, many will retire. The next generation, Generation X, with 15 million fewer members, doesn't have the critical mass to fill their shoes, much less new job openings. The generation after that, Generation Y—now ranging in age from babies to college students—is larger, so it will partly alleviate the labor crunch. But Gen Y workers are also likely to follow form and be better educated than their elders, which will push them toward high skill careers. Immigrants will still be needed if the U.S. economy is to continue growing.

> "The current demographic situation—a high supply of Mexican migrants and high demand for them from U.S. employers—inexorably reflects the laws of supply and demand. Sealing our borders won't change that now or help us adjust to changing demographics and labor markets in the future."[6]

The overall views and perceptions of Latinos are mostly positive, according to a national 2006 Pew Hispanic Center Survey Report. The survey report stated the public's overall impressions of recent immigrants to the U.S. from Latin America and Asian nations "are generally positive, and nearly half of the public believes immigrants of today are just as willing to assimilate as those from a century ago."[7] However, there tends to be misinformation regarding language and immigration status of the Hispanic population: "a majority express the view that new immigrants do not learn English fast enough and pluralities believe that most immigrants today are here illegally."[8] Both statements are incorrect. U.S. Census data shows that the vast majority of the Hispanics residing in the United States are U.S. citizens or legal residents. Similarly, the growth of English-language proficiency and usage has increased dramatically the past decade, also a topic discussed later in this book.

The latter survey by Pew was conducted right at the onset of the immigration debate, which continues.

Notes

1   Mendoza, Henry and Robert Montemayor. *Right Before Our Eyes: Latinos Past, Present & Future*. Tempe: Scholarly Publishing, 2004.

2   NALEO, 1998.

3   Rios, Diana and Federico Subervi. "Latino Identity & Situational Latinidad." *Hispanic Marketing & Public Relations*. Ed. Elena del Valle. Boca Raton: Poyeen Publishing, 2005.

4   Kravetz, Carl. "Latino Identity." Paper presented September 20, 2006. The repost can be obtained at AHAA's website, *www.AHAA.org*.

5   Falicov, Celia Jaes. "Ambiguous Loss: Risk and Resilience in Latino Immigrant Families." *Latinos: Remaking America*. Ed. M. Suarez-Orozco and M.M. Paez. DRCLAS/California, 2002.

6   O'Neil, Shannon. "Will We Have Enough Workers?" *The Los Angeles Times*. April 5, 2007.

7   Ibid.

8   Pew Research Center for the People and the Press. "America's Immigration Quandary." March 30, 2006.

CHAPTER 4

Latinos in Society

Why is growth in the Hispanic population valuable to U.S. business and the country in general? As discussed in Chapter 1, overall U.S. population growth is fairly flat and the median age is projected to rise, with well-documented social, labor, and business consequences. For example, steep labor force shortages can be highly detrimental to manufacturing, services, and the marketplace. Expansion of the U.S. Hispanic population contributes to the population growth in the younger age segments in many states. This is a highly valuable "human" asset that economists in aging countries around the world, such as the U.S. and countries in Western Europe, are welcoming.

All projections show that Hispanic market growth will continue for several reasons.

- Latinos have higher fertility rates than non-Hispanic women, with an average of 98 births per 1000 women of childbearing age in 2004. White, non-Hispanic women had an average of 58.5 births per 1000 women of childbearing age.[1]

- Immigration from Mexico and Central and South America continues to be strong; most of it legally to join family members or with work visas.

- Newly arrived immigrants are historically younger than the overall population, adding to the family-formation age group, and as mentioned above, an important asset to the nation, particularly if they have access to education and achieve higher education diplomas. This is a challenge today!

Educational Attainment

In October 2004 (latest available data), 12.5 million Hispanics, approximately 32.4 percent of the Hispanic population, were enrolled in school, including nursery, kindergarten, elementary, high school, and college. Of those enrolled, 12.4 percent were enrolled in a nursery or kindergarten program, 49.4 percent in elementary school, 22.3 percent in high school, and 15.8 percent in college. This distribution of enrollment is similar to that of the population in general.

The share of Hispanic children in the educational system is rising faster than other cultural groups due to the larger number of Latinos in young age groups, the overall higher fertility rates among Hispanic women, and ongoing immigration. Presently, immigration has the greatest effect. Among Hispanic school-age children in 2003, 61 percent were U.S. born but had at least one foreign-born parent. Most Hispanic children aged 7 to 15 are enrolled in school, but there is a noticeable drop-off after age 16 when children in most school districts are legally allowed to leave school.

FIGURE 4.1 . . . .

Enrollment of Hispanics Aged 3 and Over, October 2004

(in thousands)

Nursery or Kindergarten	1,556
Elementary	6,184
High School	2,793
College	1,975
Total	12,508

Source: U.S. Census Bureau. "Educational Attainment of the Population 15 Years and Over, March 2004." Released March 2005.

The numbers may be growing as more Latino children enter the educational system; however, two serious challenges have a negative impact. First, the increasing drop-put rates, and second, the low achievement levels these—and other minority students—are showing.

FIGURE 4.2 . . . .

Hispanic Educational Attainment by U.S.-Born and Foreign-Born Generations age 25 and over, 2005

(in thousands)

	LESS THAN 9TH GRADE	9TH TO 12TH GRADE	HIGH SCHOOL GRADUATE	SOME COLLEGE	COLLEGE GRADUATE
Total Hispanic	5,446 (24.0%)	3,742 (16.5%)	6,121 (27.0%)	4,577 (20.2%)	2,785 (12.3%)
U.S.-born Hispanic/2nd Generation, 3rd Generation, and Greater	932 (9.8%)	1,432 (15.0%)	2,919 (30.6%)	2,748 (28.8%)	1,504 (15.8%)
Foreign-born/First-generation Hispanic	4,513 (34.4%)	2,311 (17.6%)	3,202 (24.4%)	1,829 (13.9%)	1,281 (9.8%)
Total U.S	11,790 (6.2%)	17,990 (9.5%)	55,907 (29.6%)	51,865 (27.5%)	51,378 (27.2%)

Note: "College graduate" refers to a person who has attained at least a bachelor's degree.

Source: Pew Hispanic Center. "Hispanics at Mid-Decade." Tabulations of 2005 American Community Survey.

U.S.-Born and Foreign-Born Hispanics and Education

As shown in Figure 4.2 above, over half of foreign-born Hispanics do not have a high school diploma. Given that many of these 1st generation immigrants came to the U.S. as adults, this is not surprising. While the percentages of Hispanics finishing high school and attending college promise to improve as the size of the 2nd and 3rd generation populations grow, it is important to recognize that children of parents who did not graduate high school or attend college are less likely to graduate high school or attend college themselves. As you will see in Latino Labor in Crisis later in this chapter, this is a looming problem for the U.S. and its ever-more skill-based labor market.

FIGURE 4.3 . . . .

Students Below Basic National Achievement Levels in Math and Reading, 2005

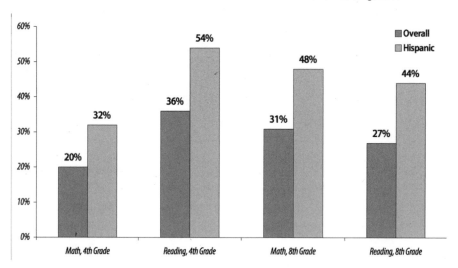

Source: National Center for Education Statistics. "The Nation's Report Card: Reading 2005" and "The Nation's Report Card: Mathematics 2005."

According to a 2005 study by the Pew Hispanic Center, 45 percent of Hispanic high school students aged 15 to 17 are below their grade level. The annual dropout rate of 7.1 percent for Hispanics in the tenth to twelfth grades is higher than among any other ethnic group.

Similar to African Americans, Latino high school graduation rates are very low, particularly among males; only 48 percent of male Hispanics enrolled in school graduate, while 58 percent of Latinas do. This situation is going to have a serious impact if it is not remedied now.

FIGURE 4.4 . . . .

High School Graduation Rates, 2004

RACE/ETHNICITY	NATIONAL	FEMALE	MALE
All Students	68.0%	72.0%	64.1%
Hispanic	53.2	58.5	48.0
White	74.9	77.0	70.8
Black	50.2	56.2	42.8
American Indian	51.1	51.4	47.0
Asian/Pacific Islander	76.8	72.0	64.1

Source: Orfield, Gary, Daniel Losen, Johanna Wald, and Christopher B. Swanson. Losing Our Future: How Minority Youth are Being Left Behind by the Graduation Rate Crisis. Cambridge, MA: The Civil Rights Project at Harvard University.

Workforce expert Dr. Carol D'Amico makes a compelling case study of the severe skills and achievement gaps among the future U.S. work force in her paper, "Workforce 2020 and Beyond: Root Causes of U.S. Workforce Challenges" (2006). D'Amico shows that despite recent improvements, Latino educational attainment remains poor. Among Hispanics aged 18 to 24 in 2004, only about 50 percent were high school graduates, of which only about 20 percent had received some college education. However, as discussed in more detail below, Hispanics tend to start college later than their non-Hispanic peers.

The College Gap

Of the 17.4 million college students enrolled in the U.S. in 2004, 11.4 percent were Hispanic. If you consider that few of these students' parents had the opportunity to go to school beyond a few grades, it is miraculous that so many Hispanic children manage to make it through the school system at all. As a foreign-born parent of two young adults in the educational system, I am aware how difficult and expensive it can be to help children successfully apply to and graduate from college and graduate school. I often asked myself, "How do less advantaged Latino families cope when trying to help their children achieve academic success in the U.S. educational system?" Hence, it is encouraging to see improvements in Hispanic educational attainment. However, much more improvement is needed.

FIGURE 4.5 . . . .

College Enrollment by Race, Fall 2004

Hispanic	**11%**
Black	13%
White, Non-Hispanic	70%
Asian, Pacific Islander, and other	6%

Source: U.S. Census Bureau

About 63 percent of Hispanics who were in college in October 2004 were aged 16 to 24, considered "traditional" ages for higher education. However, as mentioned above, more Hispanics are also enrolling in college at later ages. Just over 23 percent of Hispanic college enrollees were aged 25 to 34 in 2004, and 13.7 percent were aged 35 and older. Of the 1.9 million Hispanic students aged 15 and over enrolled in college in 2004, 35.4 percent were enrolled part-time; 49.6 percent of full-time students were also employed either full or part-time while going to school. Among part-time students, nearly 82 percent are employed, the majority full-time. Full-time employment of Hispanic students was the highest among any cultural group attending college.

This tendency to go to college later, or not at all, is reflected in Figure 4.6, below. By age 24, about 32 percent of white, non-Hispanics have at least started college. In contrast, only 20 percent of Hispanics have started college then.

FIGURE 4.6 . . . .

Educational Attainment of 18-to 24-Year-Olds by Race, 2004

	NO HIGH SCHOOL DIPLOMA	HIGH SCHOOL DIPLOMA	SOME COLLEGE	COLLEGE GRADUATE
Hispanic	**52.4%**	**26.3%**	**14.3%**	**7.0%**
Asian	44.2	12.3	32.6	10.9
Black	53.7	24.3	19.1	2.9
White, Non-Hispanic	46.3	20.4	26.5	6.8

Source: U.S. Census Bureau. "Educational Attainment of the Population 15 Years and Over, March 2004." Released March 2005.

Despite the challenges, there are noticeable improvements and awareness in the Latino community that college is important to success in the U.S.

Several websites now feature links to educational sites, quarterly chats with education experts and role models, clubs for mothers to get support on preschools from other parents, and links to relevant sites for high school students interested in pursuing higher education.

Many corporations are building their "Share of Heart" with the Hispanic market by contributing to scholarship funds and providing support for schools and colleges to create solutions to the educational challenges facing the Latino community.

As U.S. baby boomers age and become increasingly eligible for public entitlement programs such as Social Security and Medicare, Latinos will represent a significant and growing percentage of the U.S. labor force. This simple fact should entice local and national governments, educators, corporations, and community organizations to make Latino education a top priority. Despite improvements in educational attainment, high school students of Hispanic origin continue to have more problems in school.

Latinos in the Labor Force

The Bureau of Labor Statistics reports that Hispanics now account for about 13 percent of the civilian labor force, compared with just 7.4 percent in 1988. Hispanic men participate in the labor force at greater rates than white and black men. However, Hispanic women are slightly less likely than either white or black women to be employed outside the home.

FIGURE 4.7 . . . .

Labor Force and Employment Status, Aged 16 and Up, 2004

	HISPANIC		WHITE, NON-HISPANIC		OTHER, NON-HISPANIC	
	MALE	FEMALE	MALE	FEMALE	MALE	FEMALE
in labor force	79.6	55.6	72.4	59.4	67.7	60.6
Unemployed	7.5	7.9	5.7	4.4	9.8	8.5

Source: U.S. Census Bureau. Current Population Survey, Annual Social and Economic Supplement 2004. Ethnicity and Ancestry Statistics Branch, Population Division.

Hispanics have broadened their workforce participation, moving into more management and professional positions. However, as mentioned earlier, there is still a lag behind African-Americans and whites, likely because of lower educational attainment and shortage of skills overall. Among Hispanic men in the labor force in 2004, only 31 percent of those aged 25 and older had more than a high school diploma, compared with 65 percent of white men and 53 percent of black men. Among women in the labor force in 2004, 41 percent of Hispanic women aged 25 or older had more than a high school diploma, compared with 66 percent of white women and 56 percent of black women. Note that among all groups, women in the labor force aged 25 and older are more likely than men in the same age group to have more than a high school diploma.

FIGURE 4.8 . . . .

Civilian Labor Force by Race and Hispanic Origin, 1998 and Projected 2008

(total, 16 and older, in thousands)

	1998	2008 PROJECTED	CHANGE 1998–2008
Black	15,982	19,101	19.5%
Hispanic origin	14,317	19,585	36.8
Asian and other	6,278	8,809	40.3
White	115,415	126,665	9.7

Source: Fullerton, Howard N. "Labor force projections to 2008: Steady growth and changing composition." Monthly Labor Review, November 1999. Page 20, Table 2.

FIGURE 4.9A .. . .

Distribution of Second Generation Aged 25 to 54 Years by Race and Hispanic or Latino Ethnicity

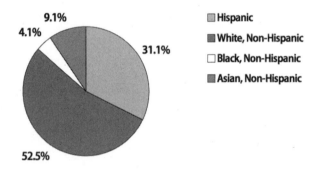

FIGURE 4.9B

Distribution of Third Generation and Greater Aged 25 to 54 Years by Race and Hispanic or Latino Ethnicity

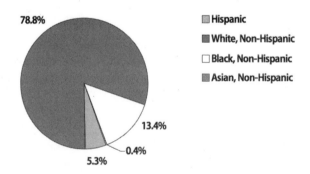

Source: "Labor Force Characteristics of Second Generation Americans," *Monthly Labor Review.* September 2006

Labor Force Participation Rates of Second and Third or Higher Generation
U.S.-Born Hispanics

March 2005

TOTAL		MEN		WOMEN	
2nd Generation	3rd Generation and Higher	2nd Generation	3rd Generation and Higher	2nd Generation	3rd Generation and Higher
82.8%	78.8%	90.5%	85.5%	75.2%	72.5%

Source: "Labor Force Characteristics of Second Generation Americans," *Monthly Labor Review.* September 2006

Latino Labor in Crisis

The composition of the U.S. workforce is changing rapidly, and according to several indicators, Latinos and African Americans have the potential to play a greater role.

Worker Gap: Future U.S. Workforce Composition

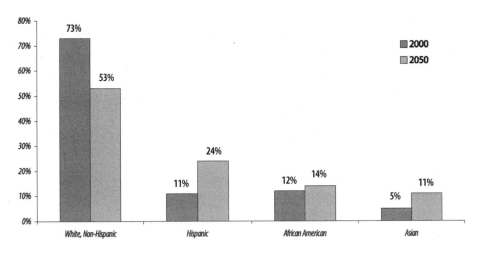

Source: D'Amico, Carol. "Workforce 2020 and Beyond: Root Causes of U.S. Workforce Challenges." Ivy Tech Community College of Indiana, 2006.

According to the "Workforce 2020" report, there will be 19 million more jobs than workers in the U.S. by the year 2008, and 40 percent of the pool of people to fill these jobs will be Latinos, African Americans, and other "minority" workers. However, the same report states that there will be an estimated

14 million-person shortage in post-secondary educated workers by 2020, and a 7 million-person shortage of non-college educated workers.

Basic skills such as reading, writing, and math are lacking among U.S. minorities while U.S. employers are demanding a higher level of skill for jobs that previously did not require post-secondary education.

For example, 17-year-old Latino and African-American students are at the same level in math as 13-year-old white non-Hispanics on average, and the case is similar with their reading skills. Needless to say, the future of the U.S. workforce is in danger, and Latinos as well as African Americans will need the required skills if a crisis is to be averted.

FIGURE 4.12 .. ..

Skills Gap: Lack of Qualified Workers

percent of workers without a college education

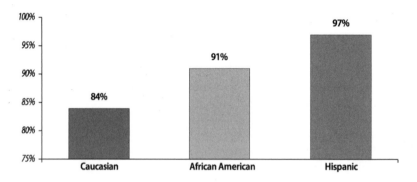

Source: D'Amico, Carol. "Workforce 2020 and Beyond: Root Causes of U.S. Workforce Challenges." Ivy Tech Community College of Indiana, 2006.

Hispanic Health and Health Insurance

Hispanics have the highest uninsured rates of any racial or ethnic group within the United States (Figure 4.13). This lack of insurance, and thus often preventative care, has led to higher mortality rates for Hispanics from a variety of afflictions. According to the Office of Minority Health, Hispanic/Latino profile:

- Hispanic men and women have higher incidence and mortality rates for stomach and liver cancer.

- Mexican-American adults were two times more likely than non-Hispanic white adults to have been diagnosed with diabetes by a physician.

- In 2003, Hispanics were 1.5 times more likely as non-Hispanic whites to die from diabetes.

- In 2003, Mexican-American men were 30 percent less likely to die from heart disease, as compared with non-Hispanic white men.

- Hispanic men were 2.7 times more likely to die from HIV/AIDS as non-Hispanic white men.

- Hispanic women were 4.5 times as likely to die from HIV/AIDS as non-Hispanic white women.

This represents both a crisis in the Hispanic community, but also an opportunity for health insurance providers. Indeed, new data released in 2007 show that 34 percent of Hispanics do not have health insurance coverage, making them the least-covered ethnic group.

The Political Scene

Hispanics are getting the message that their vote matters. At the time of the 2004 election, 9.3 million Hispanics were registered to vote, representing 7.4 percent of all registered voters. This represented a 20.4 percent increase from 2000.[2] However, their numbers are still significantly behind the 75 percent of eligible non-Hispanic whites and 69 percent of eligible blacks who were registered to vote.

According the U.S. Census, a lower percentage of registered Hispanics voted than did any other ethnic group, with 81.5 percent of registered Hispanics voting in 2004, compared with a national average of 88.5 percent of all registered voters.

FIGURE 4.14 .. ..

Hispanic Party Identification, 2004

Q. In politics today, do you consider yourself a Democrat, Republican, or something else?

	REPUBLICAN	DEMOCRAT	INDEPENDENT	SOMETHING ELSE	DON'T KNOW	REFUSED
All Hispanics	14%	35%	26%	12%	12%	2%
Registered Voters	20%	45%	21%	8%	5%	2%
Citizens, not Registered	7%	37%	24%	17%	10%	4%
Non-citizens	10%	23%	33%	14%	18%	3%

Source: Pew Hispanic Center/Kaiser Family Foundation. The 2004 National Survey of Latinos: Politics and Civic Participation.

The 2000 election was the first time in which political commentators seriously analyzed and re-analyzed the Hispanic vote and its effect on both

Democrats and Republicans. It is estimated that the two major presidential candidates, Al Gore and George W. Bush, together spent about $5 million to campaign in Spanish in their 2000 electoral bids. "This was without precedent," said to Sergio Bendixen, president of Hispanic Trends in an interview in January 2001.

However, studies by the Tomás Rivera Policy Institute show that an increase in Hispanic registered voters is not reflected equally in actual voting. Total Hispanic voter participation remains low.

As is shown in Figure 4.14, party affiliation among Hispanics is skewed. In 2001, among roughly 5,000 elected Hispanic officials whose party was known, 1,474 were Democrats and 126 were Republicans. However, there were also 2,283 elected officials whose parties were not listed and 1,309 who were elected to non-partisan offices such as school boards.

FIGURE 4.15 ....

Hispanic Party Characterization, 2004

Q. Which party do you think has more concern for Latinos—the Democratic Party, the Republican Party, or is there no difference?

	DEMOCRATIC PARTY	REPUBLICAN PARTY	NO DIFFERENCE	DON'T KNOW	REFUSED
All Hispanics	34%	9%	46%	9%	1%
Registered Voters	43%	11%	42%	4%	< 1%
Citizens not Registered	36%	5%	46%	11%	3%
Non-citizens	25%	10%	51%	14%	< 1%

Source: Pew Hispanic Center/Kaiser Family Foundation. The 2004 National Survey of Latinos: Politics and Civic Participation.

The National Association of Latino Elected Officials (NALEO), which collects data on Hispanics who are elected to office in the United States, cautions against the usage of their reports to make comparisons with prior years. The table below shows NALEO's numbers for 2005, which include a total of 5,041 elected officials by level of government. The good news is that the number of representatives in state legislatures appears to be growing and it is from this group that candidates for the U.S. House of Representatives often emerge. This suggests that we will see a growing number of Latino elected officials in coming years.

Just as in the consumer marketplace, there are differ-ences in Hispanic political attitudes in various parts of the United States depending on degree of acculturation. For example, foreign-born Hispanic voters who tend to get their information from Spanish-language television vote differently than those who have access to English-language media. Moreover, different cultural issues can affect voter turnout and results. In Florida in 2000, it is believed that Cubans turned out to vote against Al Gore to protest the Clinton administration's handling of the Elián González case of the shipwrecked boy who was returned to his Cuban father. Some analysts say this extraordinary growth in Cubans voting Republican rather than Democratic is what confused pollsters about the outcome of the Florida election. In the interim elec-tions in 2005, the immigration issue may have had a sig-nificant impact on contests in Arizona, New Mexico, and California. In the 2008 Presidential Election, the immi-gration issue will likely loom large.

FIGURE 4.16 .. ..

Hispanics in Government, 2005

LEVEL OF OFFICE	NUMBER
Governor	1
Senators	3
U.S. Representatives	22
State legislators	232
State officials	8
County officials	498
Municipal officials	1,651
Judicial/Law Enforcement	678
Education/School board	1,760
Special District officials	188
Total	5,041

Source: NALEO Educational Fund. 2005 National Directory of Latino Elected Officials.

While Hispanic voter influence should continue to grow, some analysts worry that a higher cost in government naturalization fees may discourage some immigrants from becoming citizens. In that case, the growth in Hispanic voting power might slow down. As one might guess, this issue is at the top of Hispanic politicians' and lobby groups' agendas.

Hispanics in Business

Along with the impressive growth in the population and buying power of American Latinos (see Chapter 1), there has also been significant growth in their business involvement. Not only are Hispanics consumers of mass-market goods, but they also contribute greatly to the marketplace as entrepreneurs and producers of goods and services. For companies targeting businesses, Latinos are creating new firms at a rapid pace! Unfortunately, data from the U.S. govern-ment does not keep pace with this growth. The table below shows the top 20 states with the largest number of Hispanic-owned firms in 2004, but this is a projection based on data from 1992 to 1997.

FIGURE 4.17 .. ..

Twenty States with the Largest Number of Hispanic-owned Firms, 2004

	FIRMS	% OF TOTAL FIRMS	SALES (IN US$ BILLIONS)	% OF TOTAL SALES	AVERAGE SALES
1. California	713,182	35%	85.6	31%	$119,963
2. Florida	357,208	17	67.1	24	$187,741
3. Texas	299,938	15	23.3	9	$77,825
4. New York	151,626	7	16.2	6	$107,076
5. New Jersey	65,379	3	12.6	5	$192,079
6. Illinois	55,406	3	7.5	3	$135,193
7. Arizona	38,585	2	5.2	2	$134,464
8. New Mexico	33,294	2	3.1	1	$94,012
9. Virginia	31,990	2	3.6	1	$111,613
10. Maryland	27,554	1	3.2	1	$114,460
11. Massachusetts	25,074	1	2.4	>1	$94,588
12. Georgia	22,665	1	4.2	2	$184,922
13.Colorado	21,414	1	4.2	2	$196,241
14. Washington	16,964	>1	3.5	1	$203,931
15. Connecticut	14,804	>1	1.7	>1	$117,141
16. Pennsylvania	13,285	>1	3.3	1	$247,432
17. Nevada	13,176	>1	2.2	>1	$168,883
18. Michigan	11,839	>1	2.5	>1	$209,719
19. North Carolina	11,336	>1	2.5	>1	$219,486
20. Hawaii	11,088	>1	1.1	>1	$98,950

Source: HispanTelligence® Market Brief, June 2004. Projections based on U.S. Economic Census SMOBE data for 1992-1997, used by permission.

Corporate Influence

Beyond owning their own businesses, Hispanics also have increasing influence in corporations and their boardrooms.

In their June 2007 corporate governance study, HACR (the Hispanic Association for Corporate Responsibility) summarizes the status of Hispanics in Fortune 500 boardrooms:

- Since 2003 there has been a 26 percent rise in the number of Hispanics sitting on Fortune 500 boards.

- Almost 10 percent of Fortune 500 boards have maintained Hispanic representation for at least a decade.

- Hispanics held just 3.1 percent of all Fortune 500 board seats in 2006.

- Hispanic women held just 0.8 percent of all Fortune 500 board seats in 2006.

- Almost three times as many Hispanics serve on Fortune 500 boards than on Fortune 501-1000 boards.

- The number of Hispanics serving as board chairs, presidents, and/or CEOs in the Fortune 1000 has increased from 16 to 22.

- Just two companies in the Fortune 5000 had three or more Hispanic board members.

- Only 1 percent of executive officer positions were held by Hispanics.[3]

Latinos in Management

FIGURE 4.18 .. ..

Occupational Distribution of Second- and Third-Generation and Higher U.S.-Born Hispanics, March 2005

	SECOND GENERATION			THIRD GENERATION AND HIGHER		
	MEN	WOMEN	TOTAL	MEN	WOMEN	TOTAL
Management, Business, and Financial Operations	10.5%	14.4%	12.3%	12.5%	12.9%	12.7%
Professional and Related	13.7	25.7	19.2	12.7	20.8	16.5
Service	15.6	15.5	15.6	16.1	21.9	18.8
Sales and Office	22.0	38.7	29.6	17.3	37.4	26.8
Natural Resources, Construction, and Maintenance	17.5	0.7	9.8	19.3	0.8	10.6
Production, Transportation, and Material Moving	20.7	5.0	13.5	22.2	6.2	14.6

Source: "Labor Force Characteristics of Second-Generation Americans." *Monthly Labor Review.* September 2006.

Latinas are significantly more active in the managerial workforce than their male counterparts. Among Hispanic men in the labor force in 2004, 13.2 percent held managerial or professional positions, compared with 29.2 percent of non-Hispanic white men and 18.5 percent of black men. Among women, 27.8 percent of Hispanics were managers or professionals, compared with 33.4 percent of non-Hispanic whites, and 24.8 percent of blacks.

As expected, education has a significant impact on earnings. In 2005, according to the Pew Hispanic Center, the median personal earnings for full-time, year-round Hispanic workers (who worked at least 48 weeks and 35 hours a week in the past year) was $25,100, compared with $40,000 for non-Hispanic whites and $30,000 for non-Hispanic blacks. The earnings gap is larger for Hispanic men than for Hispanic women, probably reflecting the higher educational levels of Hispanic women. Hispanic men earned about 62 percent of what their white counterparts earned, whereas Hispanic women earned about 72 percent of what their white counterparts earned. Since 1986, the earnings gap between Hispanics and their white counterparts has widened. Among workers paid hourly rates, there was little difference between Hispanics, whites, and blacks in the proportion who worked at or below the prevailing minimum federal wage in 2000.

Growth in the Hispanic labor force is projected by the Bureau of Labor Statistics to continue for the near future. By 2008, the Hispanic labor force is projected to overtake the black labor force in size, primarily as a result of continued immigration. Labor force participation rates for Hispanics are projected to remain virtually the same.

Hispanic Banking

The Hispanic banking market has great opportunity for growth for two reasons: First, relatively few U.S. Hispanics currently have a bank account, due in part to their youth, but also due to the fact that many banks were unwilling or unable to connect with Hispanic consumers in-culture. According to market researcher Simmons, Inc., in 2005, 56 percent of U.S. Hispanics had never held a bank account.[4] Second, a large percentage of the Hispanic population will be moving into their prime earning years in the next decade. The FDIC predicts that Hispanics will account for more than 50 percent of retail banking growth, about $200 billion dollars, in the next 10 years.[5]

Recently, some banks have begun to court the Hispanic market more aggressively. According to a *BusinessWeek* story, "At Bank of America, Spanish-language advertising brought in 1 million new checking accounts from Hispanics last year—fully 25 percent of the new accounts opened."[6]

Another bank that has started to develop the Hispanic market is Promerica Bank in Los Angeles. Maria Contreras Sweet, founder, says:

"As the first Latino bank in Los Angeles in over 30 years, we continue to make history. I am pleased to report that your first Promerica Bank shareholder meeting was well-attended and very informative. I was delighted to share the wonderful notoriety and prestigious visitors Promerica Bank is enjoying. We hosted U.S. House Majority Leader Steny Hoyer, Governor Bill Richardson, actor Jimmy Smits, Congresswomen Lucille Roybal-Allard, and Hilda Solis to name a few. We have received awards from several members of the U.S. Congress as well as high-ranking state and local elected officials."

The lowest income brackets tend to reflect the incomes of the most recently arrived immigrants, usually single, and as mentioned earlier the U.S.-born Latino household has not kept up with the pace of household income growth of the foreign-born Latino. This may change in the near future as the "Latino Millennials" (see Chapter 8, Latino Youth) enter the labor market in the next decade with higher educational attainment.

As large as the potential Hispanic market described above is, one should bear in mind that this is just the tip of the iceberg. The many Hispanics who will open their first checking accounts in the next decade will continue to need more advanced financial services as they mature, paying huge dividends over the course of their lifetimes to the institutions who make the effort to market to them in-culture today.

Latinos and Credit Cards

With growing household incomes (see previous sections) and greater emphasis on financial services targeting Latinos, credit card ownership and usage is now common practice in most Hispanic households. The number of cards per household is at parity with the total market (see Figure 4.19); however, differences between Hispanic and non-Hispanic households are still evident. Although the median credit limit is half that of the non-Hispanic household ($6,000 vs. $12,000), the percentage of households carrying a balance is significantly higher in Hispanic households, 77 percent versus 45 percent of total households. This suggests that Latino households are disproportionately indebted, a fact that needs to be taken into consideration when targeting financial services to Hispanic households.

FIGURE 4.19 .. ..

Credit Limit and Balance of Total Households and Hispanic Households, 2004

AVERAGE AMONG THOSE WHO USE CARDS	TOTAL HOUSEHOLDS	HISPANIC HOUSEHOLDS
Number of Cards	3	3
Carry a balance*	45%	77%
Median balance	$2,380	$1,900
Median credit limit for households who reported carrying a balance	$12,000	$6,000

*NCLR calculation based NCLR data from 2004 Survey of Consumer Finances.
NCLR Issue Brief No. 17, 2007, p. 6 (www.nclr.org).

Source: Unpublished data from the 2004 Survey of Consumer Finances tabulated by the Federal Reserve on behalf of NCLR.

Latinos as Homebuyers

Home purchase is the largest expenditure for most families, and for the Latino in particular, it is the dream of a lifetime. In the U.S., home ownership is an indicator of financial success, and there is perhaps no clearer gauge of the growing importance of the Hispanic population in the U.S. economy than the increase in home ownership that has already begun and promises to accelerate in the coming years.

FIGURE 4.20 .. ..

Hispanic Housing Tenure by Foreign-Born/U.S.-Born (2nd and 3rd+ Generations), 2005

	OWNER-OCCUPIED		RENTER-OCCUPIED	
	NUMBER	%	NUMBER	%
Total Hispanic	6,063,429	48.5%	6,439,087	51.5%
U.S.-born Hispanic (2nd and 3rd+ generations)	3,024,177	52.4	2,742,683	47.6
Foreign-born/First-generation Hispanic	3,039,252	45.1	3,696,404	54.9
Total U.S.	76,665,132	66.8	38,074,711	33.2

Source: Pew Hispanic Center. "Hispanics at Mid-Decade." Tabulations of 2005 American Community Survey.

The real-estate market has experienced an increase among Hispanic homebuyers. A recent survey found that Hispanic first-time homebuyer respondents are younger than whites (mean age 30 and 34 respectively) and there was no significant income difference. The study also showed that Hispanic respondents were likely to invest larger sums for a first home ($262,000) than both white ($196,000) and African American ($215,000) respondents.[7]

Foreign-born home ownership increases with the number of years of residence in the U.S. This suggests growth potential and impact of the Hispanic homebuyer in the U.S. real-estate market. In one decade, 1990 to 2000, 34 percent of Hispanics purchased a home, and in the five years that followed (2000 to 2004), there was a similar pattern of market penetration, suggesting the Hispanic real-estate market and after market has tremendous room for growth, as fewer than half (48 percent) of Hispanics currently own a house compared with 69 percent of the total U.S. population (Figure 4.20).

FIGURE 4.21 .. ..

Hispanic Home Ownership by Foreign-Born/First Generation and Period of Arrival, 2005

PERIOD OF ARRIVAL	NUMBER OF HOMEOWNERS	% OWNING HOME
Before 1990	2,202,142	58.9%
1990 to Before 2000	699,291	34.2%
2000 and After	137,819	14.5%
Total	3,039,252	45.1%

Source: Pew Hispanic Center. "Hispanics at Mid-Decade." Tabulations of 2005 American Community Survey.

Figure 4.21 shows that the longer Hispanic immigrants have been in the country, the more likely they are to purchase a house. This fact, coupled with the large number of younger U.S. Hispanics preparing to enter the home-buying market, indicates that the real-estate market has huge potential for growth, as does the market for home furnishings.

The Tomás Rivera Policy Institute (TRPI) estimates that 1.5 million Latino households nationwide are expected to buy homes by 2010. However, TRPI also estimates that if Latinos were offered more bilingual outreach, counseling, and access to innovative mortgage products, another 700,000 Latino families, 2.2 million total, could become homeowners in that time. *Hispanic Market Weekly* projects that by 2010 Latinos will account for nearly one-third of the home buying market.

You can find up-to-date industry snapshots on the Hispanic trends in many other market segments at the *Hispanic Market Weekly* website: *www.hispanic marketweekly.com.*

| CASESTUDY | VISA USA/SAN FRANCISCO HISPANIC CHAMBER OF COMMERCE |

CO-BRANDING

Profile

Visa USA is a leading payment brand and the nation's largest payment system, enabling banks to provide their consumers and business customers with a wide variety of payment alternatives tailored to meet their evolving needs.

Visa USA is committed to increasing the choice, convenience, acceptance and security of Visa payments for all stakeholders in the payment system -- members, cardholders and merchants. Through its 13,382 member financial institutions, more than 510 million Visa-branded cards have been issued to cardholders in the United States.

Worldwide, cardholders in more than 150 countries carry more than 1 billion Visa-branded cards, accounting for more than $3 trillion in annual transaction volume in 2006. VisaNet, Visa's global processing system and the world's largest financial network, processes transactions with unparalleled reliability.

Business Challenge

Visa develops Visa web based financial literacy program in English and Spanish and seeks to provide grassroots marketing tactics to launch Visa web site.

Solution

- Visa USA hires Lopez-Negrete to manage public relations
- Visa USA, as a corporate member of the San Francisco Hispanic Chamber of Commerce (SFHCC), requests assistance to produce a press conference to introduce the web-based financial literacy program to the Hispanic community
- Visa USA designs co-branded web site with SFHCC
- SFHCC works with Lopez-Negrete to conduct outreach to local media
- SFHCC maintains on-going communication with local media contacts to ensure their participation in the press conference
- SFHCC reaches out to partnering organization, Women's Initiative for Self Employment (WISE), to provide new and seasoned business owners to participate in press conference and test-drive the web-based financial literacy program to provide user feedback to the general public. Women's Initiative for Self Employment is a nonprofit organization provides developmental programs to assist women with the formation and operation of their own companies to become more financially independent and form an average of 350 new companies annually.

CASESTUDY   VISA USA/SAN FRANCISCO HISPANIC CHAMBER OF COMMERCE

- SFHCC reaches out to local dignitaries to invite them to participate in the press conference and provide remarks

Results

- Press conference launches with the participation of the two largest Hispanic television media, Telemundo and Univision, the largest Bay Area Hispanic print media, El Mensajero, and the participation of North Bay community cable show, Encuentro Latino.

- Public Television show featured on Comcast Channel 26, Encuentro Latino, provided 30 minute presentation on the web-based financial literacy program with commentaries from Visa USA, SFHCC, and WISE participants. The show aired in Marin County three times, Sonoma County once, and Napa County once.

- Media Impressions

    1. Univision San Francisco, CA: 36,676

    2. Telemundo San Jose, CA: 22,860

    3. El Bohemio News San Francisco, CA: 180,000

    4. La Oferta Review San Jose, CA: 794,580

    5. El Observador San Jose, CA: 236,424

    6. KCBS -AM, San Francisco, CA: 200,000

    Total Media Impressions: 1,470,540

- vidaydenerosf.com averaged 100,000 web hits in the first year

- Press conference launches with the endorsement and remarks from Congresswoman Nancy Pelosi's office, Assemblyman Mark Leno, San Francisco Supervisor Fiona Ma, and San Francisco Treasurer Jose Cisneros.

Client Response

Visa's goals from the partnership were to both increase the reach of our Practical Money Skills for Life financial education program within the Latino community in the Bay Area and raise awareness of all consumers of Visa's education efforts.

Visa reached out to the SFHCC because of their reputation for being a good partner to area businesses and a trusted figure in the Latino community. Without the SFHCC, Visa's ability to effectively and credibly reach Bay Area Latinos would have been dramatically reduced.

Visa partnered and created a special co-branded Visa's site that included the SFHCC logo at the top of every page. This gave the program instant credibility. Visa then worked with SFHCC on creating a media and community outreach plan that would garner support form key elected and community officials,

CASESTUDY VISA USA/SAN FRANCISCO HISPANIC CHAMBER OF COMMERCE

as well the local news media. By bringing all of the contacts and resources of Visa and SFHCC together, the results were tremendous.

Visa agreed to launch the new web site and program at a press conference at the Latino Business Center. SFHCC secured buy-in and participation from local community and elected officials. Visa's PR firm Lopez-Negrete brought in Latino and English media outlets.

The press conference and program launch were a huge success, with significant usage of the program from the community and massive media coverage for the program. All of our goals were met and this program cemented the SFHCC as a key linchpin in our educational outreach programs in the Bay Area.

Notes

1 National Center for Health Statistics. "Total births and percentage of births with selected demographic characteristics, by race and Hispanic origin of mother." United States, final 2003 and preliminary 2004.

2 *CPS Report.* November 2004.

3 The Hispanic Association on Corporate Responsibility (HACR), a coalition of influential Hispanic national organizations in Washington, D.C. *2007 Corporate Governance Study.*

4 *Business Week.* "Tapping a Market that is Hot, Hot, Hot." January 17, 2005

5 Ibid.

6 Ibid.

7 Century 21 Real Estate LLC., *www.century21.com, www.century21espanol.com, www.cendant.com/media*

CHAPTER 5

Marketing Today and Tomorrow:
The Emotional-Cultural Paradigm

"We're in the twilight of a society based on data. As information and intelligence become the domain of computers, society will place more value on the one human ability that cannot be automated: *Emotion.** This ability will affect everything from our purchasing decisions to how we work with others. Companies will thrive on the basis of stories and myths. Companies will need to understand that their products are less important than their stories."

— Rolf Jansen, in *Marketing Genius*, by Peter Fisk (Capstone, 2006)

* MY EMPHASIS ADDED.

Emotions = E (Energy) in Motion

There is a growing body of evidence and literature that lasting marketing success is based on emotional, engaging connections with the consumers—and that this starts with their hearts, not their minds! To reach consumers' hearts, marketers must add to their standard marketing and advertising skill sets and tools, a twist to ensure that the business value proposition as well as the marketing communications strategy is emotionally engaging!

A bullet-proof way to facilitate the development of the emotional link is the In-Culture Approach, which helps identify core emotionally relevant issues across cultures and sub-cultures.

Why emotions? After much research across fields and traditions, including psychology, medicine, science, literature, and others, I've found what I believe is the best definition for our purpose in the works of a gifted multidisciplinary psychologist, Aminah Raheem, Ph.D. "I define emotions as 'an electrochemical wave phenomenon expressed through the body, involving conscious, visceral, and behavioral changes.'"[1]

She continues, "This definition allows for the observable phenomenon that an explicit emotion seems to pass through the body consciousness in a wave-like motion, with a beginning, where awareness is subtle or weak; a middle, where the feeling crests or has full expression; and an end, where the physiological effects in the body settle down. . . . A thought may cause an emotion, which in turn can bring about a whole body excitation. On the other hand, thought may persist through much of the day, without such a physiological effect."[2]

As a mnemonic to remember how relevant emotions are, and how these operate in marketing, the following "summary formula" came to me:

EMOTIONS = E (ENERGY) IN MOTION

Because marketing and advertising communications are about positive emotions and intent, I have looked deeper into the field of psychology to better grasp the issue of emotions, and positive emotions in particular. What makes an emotion a "happy, fulfilling, engaging emotion?"

The new field of Positive Psychology addresses this subject, uncovering great new insights to better understand the "quality" of emotions and the nuances that drive human beings (and "human-doings") to feel happy, more whole, and more satisfied. As Carl Jung claimed, we carry "an archetype of wholeness" within us. Thus, even in the midst of our fragmentation, stresses, and mixed emotions and anxieties, "something pushes us toward whole-ism."[3]

One of the founders of Positive Psychology, Martin E.P. Seligman, Ph.D., a trail blazer in this field, describes this in one of his books: "Positive psychology is about the meaning of those happy and unhappy moments, the tapestry they weave, and the strengths and virtues they display that make up the quality of your life." "Feelings," he continues, "are states, momentary occurrences that need not be recurring features of our personality. Traits, in contrast to states, are either negative or positive characteristics that recur across time and different situations, and strengths and virtues the positive characteristics that bring about good feeling and gratification. Traits are abiding dispositions whose exercise makes momentary feelings more likely." For example . . . the positive trait makes the momentary trait of being humorous makes the state of laughing more likely."

He describes the quality of happiness, and why today's "hedonism" fails to provide that lasting, "whole and deep satisfaction of fulfilled joy," or happiness, rapture, comfort and ecstasy. "Positive emotion alienated from the exercise of character leads to emptiness, to lack of authenticity, to depression, and, as we age, to the gnawing realization that we are fidgeting until we die." We want to feel entitled to our positive feelings. Yet we have invented myriad shortcuts to feel-ing good, to happiness (from chocolate and food, drugs, loveless sex, shopping, etc.) that leave us feeling empty and emotionally starving at the end of the day. Dr. Seligman does not advocate against these short cuts altogether. However, he makes a compelling case in favor of the exercise of kindness and compassion as the most powerful short cut to positive emotions. It is beyond the scope of this book to dwell further on this subject; however, I highly recommend it as a resource to study and manage emotions in marketing communications.

Emotional marketing has been a part of the Hispanic marketing industry for some time! Chapter 6, *Share of Heart*, presents this philosophy developed by Norma and Hector Orci, pioneers in emotional advertising.

FIGURE 5.1 . . . .

Building the U.S. Hispanic Marketing Industry

Hispanic Marketing Paradigm

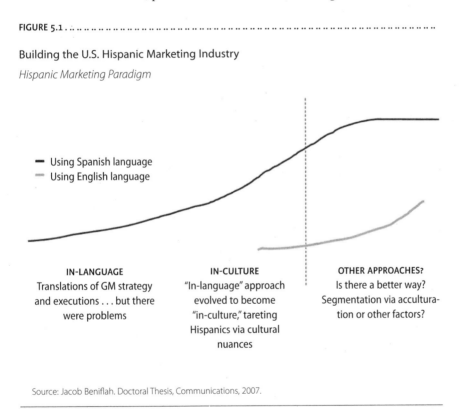

- Using Spanish language
- Using English language

IN-LANGUAGE	IN-CULTURE	OTHER APPROACHES?
Translations of GM strategy and executions . . . but there were problems	"In-language" approach evolved to become "in-culture," tareting Hispanics via cultural nuances	Is there a better way? Segmentation via accultura-tion or other factors?

Source: Jacob Beniflah. Doctoral Thesis, Communications, 2007.

Based on the Share of Heart philosophy we developed the In-Culture Approach to bring to life culturally-attuned business models and marketing communication strategies with messages that deliver emotionally engaging, motivating concepts through every stage of the business plan and contact with the consumer. The ideal result of this strategy is to generate "moving" ideas to entice consumers to "fall in love" with your brand, products, and/or services.

The In-Culture Approach: Building HeartShares for Lasting MarketShares

The well-developed in-culture marketing strategy connects with the consumer as a "whole person," 360 degrees, considering and talking to their hearts and minds and capitalizing on their unique culture. The aim is to build HeartShares, to be "loved" by the consumer, in order to gain lasting MarketShares.

The "in-culture" marketing concept emerged in the mid 1980s and 1990s from the original methodologies developed at Hispanic Market Connection, Inc. (HMC), my former company, whose first slogan was, *"It's not a matter of language but culture."* The In-Culture Approach evolved in response to clients' needs for deeper multicultural[*] marketing intelligence and consumer insights. The definition has changed over time. This is my most recent iteration:

> In-Culture Marketing is a method that recognizes that the growing number of consumer segments experience life in a different cultural context than that of mainstream society (e.g., America); hence, their value orientation, history and myths, needs, wants, expectations, beliefs, purchasing behavior, forms of interactions, lifestyles, etc., tend to differ from those of the average mainstream culture.
>
> In-Culture Marketing recognizes the existence, capitalizes on and builds upon these cultural differences to bring the consumer to your product, service and brand—integrating every aspect of the business model, from value proposition, product development, execution, marketing strategy, sales, retailing, merchandising and tracking of results.
>
> In-Culture Marketing provides a process to uncover the emotional connection of your brand and its context with the target consumer inviting them to your category and brand and keeping them as loyal, long-term and profitable clients.[4]

This chapter addresses culture, cultural issues, and the acculturation process. It also includes several tools to develop in-culture business propositions, strategies, and messages.

About Culture

Culture, and the study of cultures (and acculturation), is a rich and vast field that cannot be addressed in a few paragraphs without falling into over-simplification. Hence, please accept my descriptions of culture as a basic and simple introductory attempt to get points across in a summarized way, as pertaining to

[* ALSO REFERRED TO AS MINORITY OR "ETHNIC" MARKETING.]

marketing and business communications. For further study of culture, I recommend reviewing some of the great books, academic and non-academic papers, as well as journals and websites available that study culture or aspects of culture, in greater depth. (A bibliography is included in addition to the reference list cited at the end of each chapter.)

What is Culture?

There are over 100 definitions of culture and explanations of what culture is. For the purpose of discussing Hispanics, marketing, and acculturation, a broad definition is in order.

Culture, in broad terms, may be defined as "the system of social institutions, traditions, value orientation, and beliefs that characterize a particular social group or country and which are systematically transmitted to succeeding generations."[5] In other words, culture encompasses life at all levels—aspirations, dreams, and emotional, physical, and metaphysical behavioral traits.[1] Culture encompasses everything a person has seen, heard, and experienced from birth on—from parents, grandparents, siblings, friends, schoolteachers, media, the clergy, and so on. Culture is the depository of everything we've experienced in life since birth—from the mundane to the abstract—that gives meaning to our perceptions of people, countries, and religion, acquired in the course of our lives. We acquire these from the closest people, our parents, and family and friends, as well as the unknown and distant ones, through mass media and now, the internet.

Today we can refer to culture as the programming or software that runs our mental and emotional bodies (our RAM—random access memory—and hard drive.

In summary, we develop our "cultural software" throughout life and from many sources, with corresponding versions and upgrades as we grow up and enter the different life stages. We can "crash" parts or versions of the cultural software, and even upgrade and override components by changing our values and views of the world. However, we can never go back and replace or relive the formative years of life. Childhood and adolescence, the growing-up experiences, likes and dislikes stay in our unconscious mind forever, and emerge to our conscious awareness in most unexpected moments. However, it does operate from the unconscious most of the time! A musical tune, a scent, a flavor, even a tone of voice can prompt these old memories, fears, and pleasures to pop up. This is our cultural heritage, "the bubble" that encompasses every second of our lives. Learning how to tap into the cultural software of a different cultural segment to make business decisions and to create culturally relevant and attuned marketing and communications campaigns is the basis of In-Culture Marketing.

Acculturation: A Non-Linear Process

Upon arrival in the United States, immigrants come into contact with a different culture. They soon begin to observe that the lifestyles, customs, aspirations, and values in the new society are somewhat or greatly different from their own. What is considered a given in their home country now may be questioned, reassessed, and sometimes replaced with a different viewpoint, lifestyle, or way of doing things. As they become familiar with the traditions and the way of life in the United States, immigrants develop new approaches to interacting, living, and understanding the world around them. Slowly but steadily, the acculturation process begins and carries on. This is the acculturation process:

FIGURE 5.2 . . . .

Landscape of Acculturation Today

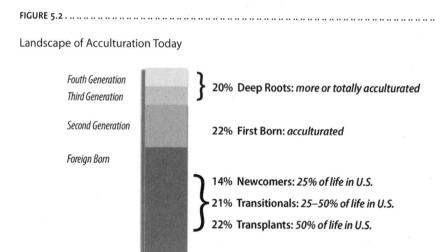

Source: Based on M. Isabel Valdés Generational Chart and Carlos Arce's Acculturation Model.

The process of acculturation takes place at all levels of social interaction (see *The Ecosystemic Model* section later in this chapter). Understanding its dynamics is critical to defining the Hispanic business opportunity, selecting your target market segments—or "sweet spot"—in-culture, and learning how to market, interact, communicate, and work with the Hispanic consumer market while acculturating. (Acculturation is described in more detail in the next section.)

Abundant research conducted over the past decades indicates identifiable Hispanic cultural traits can be found in U.S. Hispanic families even when they have resided in the United States for several generations. Studies conclude that the acculturation process can be slower or faster depending on the degree and the quality of interaction between the immigrant and members of the host country.

Because new immigrants arrive daily, the acculturation process is continuously changing and remains a moving target. While some quickly learn how to get around in the new culture, others are slowly learning the ropes, as many arrive in the U.S. and must start the process from stage zero.

In addition, the Hispanic community evolves and changes fueled in part by Hispanic culture "coming of age" with a strong demographic presence but also in business, politics, the media, the arts, and more. Advertisers and marketers need to "update" their acculturation insights continually to communicate in synch with Hispanic consumers. Ad campaigns and other marketing efforts targeting Hispanics must successfully communicate with a market that is conspicuously new, as well as one that has varying degrees of knowledge about the category or the brand.

To be effective, campaigns targeting Hispanic consumers must be engaging and emotionally moving in consonance with the Hispanic culture at all message levels: symbolic, explicit, visual, and subliminal.

Acculturation Factors

There are many external factors that play a role in acculturation, circumstances over which the person has little or no control. For example, the size of the Hispanic community or neighborhood in which Latinos grow up may either accelerate or slow the acculturation process. A neighborhood with a large Hispanic population tends to slow down the acculturation process. An individual who lives and works in a predominantly Anglo environment will probably adopt some cultural traits faster. Another external factor that affects the degree of acculturation is the level of acceptance or rejection by the community. If Hispanics are accepted and integrated into American society, rather than isolated, their chances for a faster acculturation process are greater. The acculturation pace also varies according to age. Children and adolescents have a much easier time than adults adapting to new circumstances.

Other factors affecting the nature and speed of acculturation are internal to the individual and include psychological characteristics, educational level, economic status, and the presence or absence of personal and family networks. When immigrants are educated, financially stable, surrounded by friends and family familiar with the language or an American support network, they tend to acculturate faster. Finally, some social behaviors and cultural aspects can be assimilated faster than others. For example, learning a new language is easier than adopting new values. Core cultural values and beliefs are usually difficult to change. This is true across socioeconomic groups and is independent of years of residence in the U.S. or even number of generations living in America.[7]

Foreign-born, first-generation individuals and families who move to the United States could be described as the pioneers. They tend to be more innovative and less passive than relatives who come to join them later or second-generation siblings and children who are born in the U.S.

Retro-Acculturation

Retro-acculturation, a term coined by Hispanic marketing researcher Carlos E. Garcia, refers to the conscious search for ethnic identity or roots, especially by second, third, or fourth-generation Latinos who feel they have lost their cultural identity. These individuals tend to be assimilated into mainstream American culture yet would like to enjoy and recover the culture of their parents and grandparents.

Hispanics who choose retro-acculturation typically want to learn Spanish, have their children learn Spanish, and appreciate their cultural heritage (values, music, arts, food and so on). They are proud of their heritage and welcome ethnic recognition in advertising and promotion of brands and services. As consumers, they may patronize brands that target Hispanics, or may watch Spanish-language TV and listen to Spanish-language programming. They also tend to support Hispanic-related activities, purchase Spanish-language newspapers, and vote for Hispanic candidates. A sense of ethnic identity and pride tends to motivate these behaviors. This sub-segment of the Hispanic market is growing steadily as the Latino middle class continues to grow.

Managing Cultural Differences

The "cultural divide" among Hispanics and between Hispanics and other Americans is still wide. Most Hispanic men and women arrive in the United States as adults, bringing with them the culture acquired in their Latino, non-Anglo societies. The extent to which these immigrants participate in American society affects how fast they incorporate into mainstream American culture, a process we call "acculturation."

Therefore, immigrant consumers' indigenous cultures can act as "filters" to relating or understanding mainstream advertising and communications messages that lack *cultural affinity*. This can rapidly diminish the effectiveness and sales results of a marketing campaign.

For example, some products, brands, or services may be popular with the general U.S. market because they are a part of their history growing up. However, this does not necessarily apply to the foreign-born U.S. resident or newly arrived immigrant consumers who may lack the knowledge, emotional connection, or experience with these products, brands or services.

Studies we conducted over the years have shown that depending on the country of origin, and/or the degree of urbanization of their former places of residence, recent immigrants may not be familiar with or even know about some products. For example, in one study we conducted a few years back with recent immigrants from Mexico and other countries in Central America, we learned some women in the West and Southwest washed their hair with hand soap because it is the common practice in the small town where they were raised, and according to them, "it works." However, this practice did not exist among recent immigrants who migrated from large urban areas in the same countries. Similarly, another study on infant care revealed that some Hispanic mothers continue to wrap their newborn babies tightly with a cloth to "make sure the belly button heals safely," while others did not bathe their infants until their belly buttons had healed. Some refuse to take "sitz baths" at the hospital after delivering their babies for at least two weeks. This, as we learned, was to avoid contact with impure water, a common occurrence in their native towns, and subsequently avoid infections.

These are but a few examples illustrating how Hispanic consumers from different countries can relate to or use products differently, and how important cultural affinity is in marketing communications. Messages, creative strategies, visuals, and symbols must be selected with the consumer's socio-cultural background in mind. The point is not that marketers and advertisers promote old behavior practices (e.g., not bathing an infant), but, for example, that they become aware of and have respect and understanding for the cultural differences that exist. Only then can they develop the appropriate in-culture strategy

—one that incorporates the consumer's knowledge and practices, and from that point of view introduces the new "modern" practices. This does not imply that the campaign will refer explicitly to the old practices necessarily, but present the "modern" solution addressing the benefits of the new proposed behavior from their context—in this case, "Water is always clean and safe in America; one more advantage for delivering your baby at our hospital!"

How we interact when we converse or greet each other differs by culture. What is perfectly acceptable in one culture may not be acceptable in another. Hence, to communicate memorable messages with impact, they need to be in synch with the cultural context and mindset of the target consumer. Imagine, for instance, a situation in which people from the same country converse with dear friends. They all speak the same language. Verbal language is the cultural bond easiest to observe, but it is only one of the many taking place simultaneously. For example, non-verbal behaviors (i.e. body language), shared cultural background (such as memories, events, customs, dress codes), and explicit and implicit social protocols common to people from the same social group are all examples of cultural bonds.

Verbal and non-verbal cues can vary significantly among cultures, so what makes sense to (or is "in harmony with") members of one culture may mystify members of another culture. Our cultural software is present implicitly, on a conscious and unconscious level. We tend not to be aware of its influence; we take it for granted. We assume everybody "sees the world like me." This is certainly the case when communicating with consumers of the same cultural and social group, but not always so when communicating *successfully* across cultures.

Figure 5.3 shows examples of cultural orientation differences between traditional Hispanics and the American middle class.

FIGURE 5.3 . . . .

Value Orientation Differences Between Traditional Hispanics and the American Middle Class

	HISPANICS	ANGLOS
How we see and define ourselves	As part of a family clan or group	Within ourselves, as individuals
Whom we rely on for help	Family, friends, community (Hispanic "social security")	Ourselves and institutions
What we value in people	Stress differences, show respect	Minimize differences, everybody's the same
What we stress in relationships	Respect, cooperation, formality	Symmetrical interpersonal relationships, informality, competition
Children	Dependence, obedience	Independence, egalitarian
Family	Defined roles, hierarchy, old men know more than young men	Role diffusion, democracy, younger men have a say
Sex roles in social relationships	Male dominance, machismo	Gender equality

Source: Developed by M. Isabel Valdés, 1987–2007.

Context is also relevant in the communications process. Suppose you are designing a television advertisement for a Hispanic audience and the commercial requires the presence of a minor or a woman. Can you show a Hispanic child playing alone and unsupervised in a non-family environment? Can you show a Hispanic woman drinking an alcoholic beverage alone? A yes to these questions might well result in a commercial that could backfire.

Why could it backfire? Many commercials designed for Hispanic viewers frequently reflect the lifestyles and idiosyncrasies of Anglo-American viewers. The prevalent attitude among some advertisers is that a "few adjustments here and there" are all that is needed to elicit the response of a Hispanic audience. Unfortunately, these minor adjustments overlook cultural nuances and differences. These variations may not be readily apparent to the management in a company and frequently are not detected with standardized copy testing methods or survey questionnaires. But the variations will surface when the campaign is aired—and may receive negative attention from the target audience. Ideally, campaign messages should be subjected to in-depth, unstructured qualitative probing in focus groups or one-on-one interviews with representatives of the targeted Hispanic consumer group. The following tools provide ways to check how close your thinking or strategy is to that of the core Hispanic customer. The table below (Figure 5.4) summarizes some of the "typical" cultural differences we've compiled over the years from many sources.

Broad Cultural Differences Between Working Class Hispanics and the American Middle Class

HISPANICS	ANGLOS
Group oriented ("for my family")	Self oriented ("for me")
Larger families	Smaller families
Success tends to mean family, group satisfaction	Success tends to mean personal possessions, individual satisfaction
Lean toward collectivism	Lean toward individualism
At least one daily meal involves elaborate food preparation	Daily meals are usually not prepared from scratch
Stress hierarchies, social class, social stratification, interdependence	Stress equality, equal rights, democracy, authority, symmetrical relationships, individual autonomy
Doctors and any established source of authority are respected and trusted and never questioned	Doctors and other established sources of authority may be respected and trusted but often are questioned
Believe in fate: pessimists	Believe in self-determination: optimists
Accept delayed gratification	Look for immediate gratification
"High-touch," physical closeness, hugging, affectionate	"High-tech," more physically distant
Spontaneous: Overt emotions are part of the culture	Planners: Hiding emotions is encouraged
Relaxed about time	Adhere to schedules
Very sensitive to fashion	Relaxed about fashion
Longer social protocols, indirect	Brief, to the point, and direct
Pay careful attention to clothing, appearance, and hairstyle	Far more relaxed and casual about clothing, appearance, and hairstyle
Adapt to environment	Change the environment
Low reliance on institutions	High reliance on institutions
Very decorative in homes	More casual about home decorations
Buy American products	Tend to buy imports
Value highly personal or personalized service	Value fast, efficient service at arm's length
Appreciate being given all the needed time (the more the better) when interacting with service providers	Appreciate efficiency, to the point
Rely more on mutual, implicit understanding	Rely more on explicit language
Tend to prefer known brands	Less likely to prefer prestige brands
Tend to live in larger households	Tend to have smaller households
Stress cooperation, participation, being a part of the group	Stress competition, achievement, motivation, self-competence

Source: Developed by M. Isabel Valdés, 1987–2007.

Traditional Latino Attitudes Towards Money

In traditional Latino culture, striving for money and success are not at the center of family values. As a matter of fact, a central tenet of these Latino family values is that "God loves the poor;" hence, it discourages many from thinking about money—not to mention "wealth." This is a traditional Hispanic cultural trait that has its roots in the Catholic religion (still the dominant religion among Hispanics). The Bible says, "It is easier for a camel to go through the eye of a needle than for a rich man to enter heaven." Lionel Sosa, CEO of the think tank Mexicans and Americans Thinking Together (MATT, *www.matt.org*), analyzes how Hispanic attitudes about money, success, and more are changing as the population acculturates, as shown in Figure 5.5.

FIGURE 5.5 . . . .

Old and New Attitudes Towards Traditional Hispanic Family Values

OLD ATTITUDE	NEW ATTITUDE
"Stay poor, go straight to heaven."	"It's OK to have money. It's OK to have a lot of money. God loves the poor as well as the rich."
"Drop out of school, get a job."	"Finish college, earn more, contribute more. It's a better way to help the family."
"We'll never be able to afford college, so why invite disappointment by getting ready for it?"	"Work smart and get prepared; the money will be there if you believe it will be there. Be creative and resourceful."
"Any steady job is honorable."	"Set high goals for a dream career. You are capable of achieving anything you want. Go for it. You will be successful."

Source: Lionel Sosa, excerpts of the material presented at the Tomás Rivera Policy Institute Conference. Los Angeles, May 2007.

These rich insights could be used, once tested, with target consumers to develop an in-culture, emotionally engaging strategy by addressing the "old view" indirectly and including the benefit for the family—from a positive perspective and always with respect.

Cultural vs. Socioeconomic Differences

It is important to keep in mind that "culture" is an abstract concept, a hypothetical construct that may be too broad and oversimplified when applied to an entire group of people, as it is to "Hispanics" in this case. It is usually true that a greater difference is found when the various socioeconomic classes are compared than when cultural groups are compared. It has been suggested to this author that many working-class Americans and African Americans are more closely aligned with the traditional Hispanic value orientation than with the orientation of middle-class Americans. Similarly, international research findings show the values of the predominant U.S. Hispanic culture to be closer to the working-class culture in their countries of origin (e.g., Central America, South America, and Mexico) than to the middle or upper class culture of these societies. This suggests that some cultural traits observed may be more socioeconomic than "ethnic" in nature.

For the purposes of discussing cultural differences between "Hispanic" and "non-Hispanic" market segments, the use of "culture" as a term is used here as a *catch-all* to refer to the "average" or most common denominator value orientation of each of the largest cultural groups being addressed, e.g., the "average U.S. Hispanic" and the "average, middle-class American," to help get the concept across. The author is aware these are presented in an over-simplified and generalized form. Culture within any society—or even area or social group—is far richer, complex, and has multiple variations and nuances, but such depth is beyond the scope of this book.

Shared Cultural Roots

What we call "U.S. Latino culture" today has common historic roots. During the Age of Discovery (circa 1500), Spain, and to a lesser extent Portugal, conquered large regions of the Western Hemisphere, including most of Central America, South America, the Caribbean, Mexico, and parts of what is today the United States—specifically Texas, Arizona, and California. Hence, the most common cultural features shared by nearly all Latin American countries are the Spanish language and the Catholic faith.

Other factors connect Latin American countries with Spain and Portugal as well. They include a tendency toward slower-paced economic, technological, and scientific development (Spain and Portugal were two of the last countries to join the Industrial Revolution). Latin American countries today still have large rural or semi-rural populations with little formal education and in some areas severe poverty. Most of these countries have not developed evenly, and they share in the struggle to survive and compete with more technologically and economically advanced neighbors or first-world countries, spawning a greater impetus for immigration for those in search of business advantages, technological advantages, or just a better life.

In addition, all Latin American countries were also greatly influenced by indigenous cultures, having had their own pre-Columbian civilizations. Examples include the Mayans and Aztecs in Mexico, the Incas in Peru, the Mapuches in Chile and Argentina, and the Guaranis in Paraguay, Columbia, and Venezuela. Many countries were also influenced by large immigration flows from northern and eastern Europe, Africa, and Asia during the 19th and 20th centuries. The influences of these various cultures are pervasive in the music Latinos enjoy singing and dancing to, as well as the different foods they eat, the religious and healing practices they follow, and their material goods, such as musical instruments and artifacts.

Thus, the knowledge of cultural and regional differences is valuable in the creative aspects of marketing, and it becomes very relevant when the target audience is a particular Hispanic subgroup.

Four Pillars: The Traditional Hispanic Culture

Some cultural traits, values and expressions are more prominent in the traditional Hispanic culture. I refer to these as the Four Pillars, and they include: Familismo, Machismo, Marianismo, and Chicoismo. Other cultural traits exist within the U.S. Hispanic culture as well, but they are less well represented than the "traditional" ones.

Familismo

Traditionally, the main pillar of Hispanic culture is the family, which includes the extended family of grandparents, uncles, aunts and cousins. The emphasis Hispanics place on relatives has been called *Familismo*. The family's needs and welfare take precedence over the individual member's needs. The family, as a group, is usually the first and only priority. This is reflected in the educational process within the family as well as in the family's expectations toward each other.

"Parents are viewed as being obliged to make all sorts of sacrifices for the children. As a response, the child is expected to show gratitude; for example, assuming responsibility for younger siblings and for the parents in old age. The child internalizes at an early age the overwhelming and powerful role of the parents and the family; the mother tends to define herself as an individual mostly in terms of her family. The father enjoys more freedom, but he is responsible for the respectful behavior of his children, and feels morally responsible for the behavior of the whole family."[8] Acculturating Hispanics tend to hold this particular cultural value more strongly than other cultural traits.

As the acculturation process advances both among foreign-borns who have spent most of their lives in the U.S. and their U.S.-born offspring, the traditional values are being replaced by the dominant Anglo-American value orientation and culture, as can be expected. This transition towards acculturation can be observed more markedly and deeply among U.S.-born, "New Millennials" and youth segments, as described in several sections of this book (see Chapters 1 and 9).

It is not surprising, therefore—since family is a long-lasting Latino value—that so many Spanish-language advertising strategies revolve around the family, either explicitly or implicitly.

FIGURE 5.6 . . . .

Traditional Familismo vs. Acculturated Familismo

FAMILISMO TRADITIONAL CULTURAL QUALITIES	ACCULTURATION INDICATORS
Collective, family-centered lifestyle	Family-centered, individual-friendly lifestyle
Family unity controls, dictates behavior	Family unity remains key; adapts to individual needs
Family excludes outsiders	Tolerates, accepts outsiders
Social life centers on the family	Extends to a broader social life
Face and formality are important	Flexibility in lifestyle, views, and attitudes
Space is communal/flexible	Recognizes individual privacy (own space)
Traditional stance: acceptant, dutiful	Individual stance: pursues own plans

Source: Developed by M. Isabel Valdés, 1987–2007.

Machismo

Machismo is a complex set of beliefs, attitudes, values, and behaviors about the role of men that is pervasive in the "traditional" Hispanic culture. The concept refers to the roles men fulfill according to societal rules and how they view themselves with respect to their environment and other people. It goes beyond how men treat women in stereotypically dominating ways, such as being "macho." It involves how men function as providers, protectors, and representatives of their families to the outer world. They have obligations and responsibilities to uphold the honor of family members, to deal effectively with the public sphere, and to maintain the integrity of the family unit. Machismo also refers to having socially acceptable, manly characteristics, such as being courageous, strong, and virile. The manly image includes being seen as the head of the household, but listening to and being respectful of women. This traditional role provides much more freedom for men than women with regard to sexual activity and public, social interactions.

FIGURE 5.7 . . . .

Traditional Machismo vs. Acculturated Machismo

MACHISMO TRADITIONAL CULTURAL QUALITIES	ACCULTURATION INDICATORS
Husband/wife roles defined and separate	Roles shift to sharing the tasks
Accepts husband's dominance	Evolves a partnership with husband/males/elders
Father/males/elders are sole providers	Assists husband as provider
Father is uninvolved with raising the kids	Father assists mother: gets involved with kids

Source: Developed by M. Isabel Valdés, 1987–2007.

Marianismo

Marianismo is, to some extent, the female counterpart of machismo. The term refers to an excessive sense of self-sacrifice found among traditional and less acculturated Hispanic women—the more sacrifice, the better the mother, the better the spouse—many times to the detriment of the woman. "Marianismo" is derived from Mother Mary's sacrifice for her children. This cultural trait is supported by a complex set of deeply-rooted beliefs and values that determine how Hispanic women choose to live, or better said, not to live their lives. In my decades as a researcher, I observed first-hand how Marianismo drives traditional Latina mothers' decision–making process. For example, we found that many Hispanic mothers did not go or postponed going to the doctor even when they felt sick because they "needed to take care of the children and the house." Often, the traditional Hispanic woman does not feel she has the right to ask her spouse to cover for her. In her frame of mind, this would be considered "selfish."

Marianismo runs deeper among non-acculturated Latinas. They tend not to spend money on themselves, even if it is money they earn. From a marketing perspective, these non-acculturated Latina women trail behind their male counterparts in their English-language skills since they have more limited social interactions. Our research found a higher incidence of low self-esteem and depression among non-acculturated Latinas. One study conducted for a telephone service company showed that a significant number of young immigrant Latinas in Chicago who were not allowed to leave home by their husbands spent many hours on the phone, running high long-distance and international phone bills in search of emotional support from their relatives left behind.

However, Marianismo has positive aspects in addition to the negative. These positive aspects are key to the Hispanic family. They include being a dedicated, loving, and supportive wife and mother, teaching the children Hispanic culture and religion, being a *comadre* (godmother, friend) in the community, and being highly empathetic and ready to help those in need. However, the negative aspects of Marianismo can affect Latinas growing up, and tend to breed low self-esteem and depression, which limits a Latina's personal potential.

FIGURE 5.8 . . . .

Traditional Marianismo vs. Acculturated Marianismo

MARIANISMO TRADITIONAL CULTURAL QUALITIES	ACCULTURATION INDICATORS
Does not seek for herself	Develops own life: works, studies, joins groups
Believes in the fates	Controls her own fate
Focused on serving her family	Expands the focus to the community
Time is to be used to "do her duty"	Time management and efficiency
Food expresses her love and identity	Food is an important but rational issue

Source: Developed by M. Isabel Valdés, 1987–2007.

Latina teen pregnancies and school drop outs are on the rise, and low self-esteem is rampant in lower socio-economic groups of Hispanics. In 1998, The National Coalition of Hispanic Health and Human Services Organization, which closely tracks Latino health-related issues, conducted a study among Hispanic girls aged 9 to 12 and their parents. It found that "the prevalence of health risk behaviors such as suicide attempts, substance use, and teenage pregnancy" was pervasive among Latina teens.[9]

These findings are consistent with other existing data on the subject. Living in two cultures while having to cope with stress and non-flattering feminine role models, in both the household and the community, are challenges that the new Latina teen is presently facing. A healthier image is slowly emerging and is discussed further in Chapter 8.

Chicoismo

Children and their potential better futures are usually the most cited reason for immigrating to the U.S. and sacrificing to succeed in a different country and language.

An interesting difference between mainstream American and traditional Hispanic cultures is the "intensity" of the focus in child-rearing orientations. "Children [in Hispanic families] are not believed to be capable of acting independently until they reach maturity ... regardless of the physical and emotional development of the child. This leads to parental over-concern for keeping the child close and attached to the family."[10]

This "over-concern" and familial attachment is a key Hispanic cultural value. From this germinates family clashes and stresses as Latino children long for the greater freedom and individuality their school peers experience. Talking from experience, this is a hard adjustment for the traditional Latino mother and father who do not always know what the "right behavior" is or how to enforce it. Certainly, this impacts the child's decision-making process in purchases and, hence, the marketing and advertising strategy. For example, even the most basic children's products, such as cereals and toys, benefit from including the mother (or another adult) in the creative strategy in order to close the sale more effectively in-culture.

FIGURE 5.9 . . . .

Traditional Chicoismo vs. Acculturated Chicoismo

CHICOISMO TRADITIONAL CULTURAL QUALITIES	ACCULTURATION INDICATORS
Self affirmation through her children	Pursues own aspirations, education, etc.
Protects and isolates her children	Lets go, allows outside participation

Source: Developed by M. Isabel Valdés, 1987–2007.

Avoiding Stereotypes

A stereotype is a set of generalizations about a group or category of people that is usually unfavorable, exaggerated, and oversimplified. Most stereotypes tend to emphasize negative qualities, are emotionally charged, and are difficult to change even in the face of empirical evidence.[11] Stereotypes, such as an advertising image of a Mexican wearing a sombrero and riding a burro, have the potential to irritate and disrupt the flow of healthy and effective communication between brands and consumers and should be eliminated from any marketing communications. The burro and sombrero may well communicate "Mexico" to a non-Mexican audience, but not to a Mexican or Mexican-American one. For anyone of Mexican descent living in an urban setting this image is an indirect insult, one that says, "you and your countrymen are backward." Avoid such popular stereotypes regarding Hispanic consumers to prevent delivering negatively charged messages.

To avoid falling into this trap, it is highly recommended that messages be created and communicated in-culture, free from stereotypes, myths, preconceptions, ambivalences, and potentially negative interpretations. The Latino customer must perceive the message as if he or she had designed it, causing the "they are talking to me!" phenomenon.

Latinos, like most people, dislike being labeled and pigeon-holed. When a consumer perceives an unfavorable portrayal, the immediate response is that the message was not created or executed by someone like himself. At that instant, the golden rule of successful communication—the message must be perceived to have come from "someone like me"—is broken. In a matter of seconds, the viewer's attention is diverted from the core message to the false or stereotypical image presented in the ad. As viewers become trapped in a tangle of miscommunication, they will not only miss the core message, they will most likely forget or walk away from the product and the sponsor.

Symbols used in stereotypical messages, whether images, music, or slang, are not the ones that targeted consumers would use to portray themselves or to communicate with each other. Avoiding such stereotypes is easier than it may appear. It is a two-step process. First, marketers must be aware that some of the perceptions people hold about others who may not look or speak like them do not hold up in the face of reality. Second, a "reality check" (e.g., qualitative research) with target consumers or experts is recommended.

Stereotypes about Hispanics tend to stress race, backwardness, and socio-economic issues, often placing Hispanics at the low end of the socio-economic scale. If these stereotypes were accepted at face value, one might ask, why bother targeting consumers who "have no money and no potential to make any?"

Ideally, when working with consumers of a different culture one would want to "think and feel" from the perspective of that culture. Practical tools to facilitate this process include the Ecosystemic Model and the Latino Life Cycle stages.

Visiting Latino Life Stages In-Culture

Mainstream consumers may find themselves entertaining thoughts such as, "By now I should have finished college/should be married/should have children;" "I have a good executive position even though I am still young; my father got his when he was much older;" "My daughter is dating—soon she will be married, leave home, and have children; I will become a grandparent and have a house full of empty rooms." These thoughts or similar ones reflect the life cycle-related expectations as mainstream Americans move through different stages in life.

FIGURE 5.10 . . . .

The Mexican-American and the Anglo-American Family Life Cycle Cultural Variation

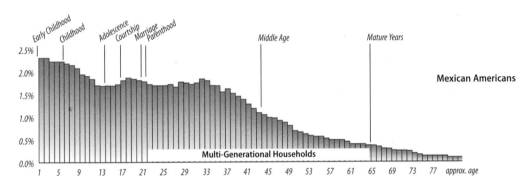

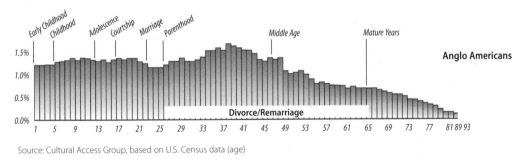

Source: Cultural Access Group, based on U.S. Census data (age)

As previously mentioned, we've been unconsciously "programmed" to expect life landmark events to take place by the time we reach a certain age. These life-cycle landmarks are "culturally" driven and hence vary between cultures. Therefore, the various events that mark the transition from one stage to another should be taken into account to develop in-culture, attuned marketing communication and campaigns for other cultures. For each stage there is a preconceived set of expectations in the consumer's mind—a commercial should match those expectations. Socially determined examples include the age a child begins school, the age at which traditional Hispanic families free their daughters of the presence of a chaperone, or the time that an oldest son is expected to begin caring for his elderly parents.

FIGURE 5.11

The Mexican-American and the Anglo-American Family Life Cycle Cultural Variation

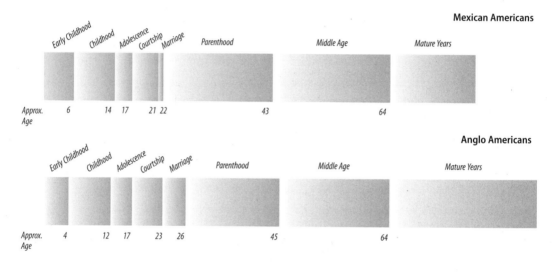

Source: Cultural Access Group,, based on U.S. Census (age); Falicov and Karrer, 1986

The life-cycle models of traditional Mexican-American and Anglo-American families are quite different. As illustrated by the life-cycle models in Figure 5.11 and Figure 5.12, relationships among traditional Mexican families tend to have longer histories. While non-Hispanics tend to spend more years in the courtship phase, it is customary for traditional Hispanics to date the same person for a long time before marriage. Hispanic couples tend to stay married longer, and Hispanic children tend to separate from their parents later than most Anglo-American children do. Traditionally, this separation did not occur until the children got married. However, acculturated young Latinas and Latinos are changing this custom in leaving for college or the workforce. For Mexican-American families, the traditional arrangements allow for greater parental intervention in their children's lives. In Mexican-American culture, there are fewer courtships, there is greater emphasis on romance, and the pressure for the families to know the bride or groom and their families is greater. To many Hispanics, courtship is a long and intense lifetime event. Hispanics also tend to divorce less often than non-Hispanics.

As a marketer, your familiarity with the events of the target audience life cycle will enhance your understanding of their attitudes and beliefs. Such awareness will improve your ability to select themes and timing that appeal to Hispanic sentiments. By choosing situations that fit into everyday Hispanic life, you gain the minds, hearts, and approval of your audience. For example, Hispanic families, on average, tend to send their children to school later than the general American population. Hispanic mothers want to keep "baby" at home for as long as possible. Therefore, a manufacturer of toys may want to capitalize on the fact that this mother will need to keep the child entertained and busy while she takes care of the household chores without the traditional help of the extended family. This mother will welcome learning practical ways to take care of the child and the household. Many ready-to-serve foods and products may also be promoted to this particular growing market segment—the Hispanic mother in child-rearing years.

FIGURE 5.12 .. ..

The Ecosystemic Model

The model shows the different levels of societal interaction, no matter what the culture.

Macrosystem: *Addresses general relationships with prototypes of ideas of the culture or subculture (ideology and myths) that set patterns for the interactions that occur at the concrete level*

Exosystem: *Addresses interactions with major institutions in society such as government, church, and media*

Mesosystem: *Addresses inter-relationships with major institutions or settings such as extended family, workplace, school peer group, and neighborhood*

Microsystem: *Addresses relationships within the family*

Source: M. Isabel Valdéz, 1991; Bronfenbrenner, U. & Falicov, C. J., 1977

FIGURE 5.13 .. .. ·

The Ecosystemic Model

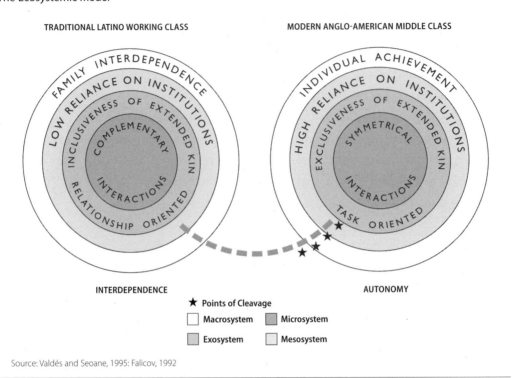

Source: Valdés and Seoane, 1995: Falicov, 1992

Unlike the lifecycle model, which views Hispanics from the perspective of the individual in his or her relation to family, the Ecosystemic Model approaches consumers from the perspective of the individual and his or her relationship to society. As the name implies, the Ecosystemic Model looks at the individual from an ecological perspective. It considers all levels or layers of society in which we operate (Figure 5.12). This model is a tool that allows one to examine how individuals from different cultures interact between, and within, the different layers of society and shows where there is room for "dissonance." Dissonance means that when the forms of interaction in a particular social layer of one culture are different from those of another culture, the doors are open to confusion, frustration, and misinterpretation. The model helps explain areas in which Hispanics are changing and adopting to different forms of interaction with their new society.

As previously mentioned, psychologists Falicov and Karrer adapted the Ecosystemic Model from one by Urie Bronfenbenner (1977) to help explain the cultural and social difficulties immigrants encounter when moving to the

United States. Even though the model was designed to represent Mexican working-class people, the author has successfully applied it to explain and uncover behavioral traits of Hispanics from other countries and socioeconomic groups. The model is described with a diagram representing traditional working-class Mexican Americans and modern middle-class Anglo Americans.

The Ecosystemic Model places the individual at the center of the circle (the Microsystem). This first circle represents the individual's interactions at the core of the family. Whereas the individual in the Anglo model tends to make decisions unilaterally, the Latino will try to make his or her decisions complement the needs of the family group.

The next layer (the Mesosystem) explains how individuals interact in the workplace, neighborhood, school, peer group, or extended family. Whereas Anglos tend to be task-oriented, Latinos will focus on the relationships.

The next layer (the Exosystem) includes the institutions that organize everyone's lives—government, business, banks, utilities, and media. Anglos tend to have a high reliance on these institutions, whereas Latinos rely on them less.

Finally, the outside layer (the Macrosystem) refers to the larger, broader, intangible layer where there are shared values, beliefs, attitudes, norms, and aspirations common to people sharing a distinct culture (Falicov and Karrer, 1986). For Anglos, individual achievement rules. For Latinos, family interdependence takes precedence.

Within each culture, there is usually consonance (tacit agreement) between the values that are practiced and the ones the culture believes in. However, between cultures (e.g., Anglo and Latino), dissonance can arise because the values of the cultures differ. As you can see in Figure 5.12, there is potential for dissonance in virtually every layer of the two cultures, but thinking about the differences helps the marketer to identify where that dissonance may occur.

How does the Ecosystemic Model work? Think of the many Hispanic immigrants who will arrive in the United States during the next ten years. Think about the Hispanic immigrants who are already here. Have you ever wondered why so many Latinos still make purchases on a cash basis and do not have checking accounts? Relative to Anglo Americans, Hispanics tend to have fewer checking accounts, make less use of financial institutions, and have fewer real-estate loans.

The Ecosystemic Model provides a framework for dealing with these types of issues. It shows how traditional working-class Latinos relate to institutions vis-à-vis middle-class Anglo Americans. Hispanics tend to rely less on institutions than do middle-class Anglo Americans. Lack of trust in institutions is a common trait among many Latin Americans. *Marketing to American Latinos: An In-Culture Approach, Part I* (Paramount Market Publishing, 2000), addresses this relationship to institutions in more detail. Any business seeking to attract Hispanic consumers should take into account the consumers' previous experience with that type of institution, service, or product.

Another example using the Ecosystemic Model can be observed at the family level. The usual forms of interaction inside the Hispanic family tend to be different than those at the heart of the American middle class. Hispanics tend to stress interdependence within the family whereas Americans tend to stress autonomy (see Figures 5.3 and 5.4). This affects, for example, how children in both cultures obtain cash to buy things they like.

In the American family, it would be perfectly acceptable for the child to find a job and earn his or her money for personal use or savings. It is actually encouraged. American children can be seen delivering newspapers, selling lemonade or cookies, and engaging in other methods of earning spending money. These activities would be unthinkable for non-acculturated, traditional Hispanic families where a child is encouraged to earn money only when the family is under severe financial stress. In the Hispanic model, it is expected that the parents provide for the children until they are young adults, continuing the tradition of long-term family interdependency. Similarly, the Hispanic mother will be responsible for the child's weekly laundry and food preparation until he or she is a young adult. Family interdependency helps explain why some Hispanic mothers continue to cook and do the laundry for their adult children, why Hispanics tend to stick together on weekends, and why parents tend to encourage their children to stay with them for as long as possible.

Many of these traits change with acculturation, and there is pressure to function in a society where the extended family is not present and, unlike in Latin America, affordable domestic help is hard to find. These behaviors and forms of interaction must be taken into consideration when marketing to non-acculturated Hispanics and should be recognized and used in the creative development process. The Ecosystemic Model lends a hand to grasp the ongoing acculturation process Hispanics and others start to go through from the moment they arrive in the United States.

Thinking in a Different Culture

Our "cultural software" determines how we are programmed to experience life. This invisible program sets up our beliefs and values, and a chain reaction begins. According to multicultural marketing expert Fons Trompenaars in his book, *Riding the Waves of Culture* (McGraw-Hill, 1997):

1. Cultural programming creates beliefs

2. Beliefs create attitudes

3. Attitudes create feelings

4. Feelings determine actions

5. Actions create results

In other words, there is a straight line between understanding the culture and getting results.

FIGURE 5.14 .. ..

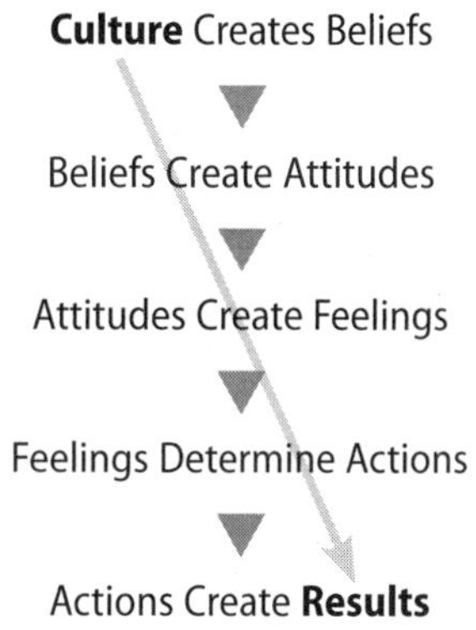

Culture Creates Beliefs

▼

Beliefs Create Attitudes

▼

Attitudes Create Feelings

▼

Feelings Determine Actions

▼

Actions Create **Results**

Source: M. Isabel Valdés Adapted from F. Trompenaars, 1997

Gaining basic insights into the specific cultural "programs" of Latinos (or other cultural groups), helps immensely in the development of successful marketing strategies. For example, societies give status to people based on different cultural "programs." Some accord status to a person on the basis of what he or she does for a living or on personal achievement. Others ascribe status based on social class, gender, education or religious background.

Latinos in Latin-American societies tend to be highly status-driven. We ascribe social status based on "who you are" (ascription)—that is, your family status, last name, wealth, etc. In comparison, Anglo-Saxons tend to ascribe status on the basis of "what you do" (achievement). Marketing managers should utilize this insight in their interactions with cultural consumers, be this in person (e.g. in a bank, hospital, or mass media) or otherwise, and should position their product or service from a perspective that reflects these cultural traits.

We have mentioned elsewhere in this and other books that the acculturation process does change value orientation and behaviors. I underscore the relevance of targeting Latinos, acknowledging generational diversity with in U.S-born and length of residence in the U.S. among foreign-born; "ascription" is a cultural trait that is easier to change by acculturation.

Sizing the business opportunity

Sizing the business opportunity in-culture requires a couple of additional questions to be added to the traditional general market questionnaire. Terry J. Soto, in her comprehensive and thorough book, *Marketing to Hispanics: A Strategic Approach to Assessing and Planning Your Initiative* (Kaplan Publishing, 2006), has synthesized the basic must-ask questions to ensure the in-culture strategic marketing approach.

Her list of questions below will ensure that you avoid some common mistakes when sizing the Hispanic business opportunity.

- "Only those Hispanics who are category users or potential category users will matter to your organization. Understanding where your target Hispanics are along the acculturation continuum based on demographics, category and brand development, attitudes and values, and psychographics is critical to determining the answer to the most important question to you and your company: What is the size of the opportunity today, and what is its potential size one, three and five years from now?"

- Are there any Hispanics in my trading area?

- How many are there?

- Where are they exactly?

- What are their general characteristics?
    - Foreign-born vs. U.S.-born
    - Country of origin
    - Length of U.S. residence
    - Language ability and use

- Media language
- Household composition
- What are their category-specific characteristics?
  - Age
  - Children in the household
  - Income

Category Development Questions

- Are Hispanics involved with the category?
- Is this a product or service—or brand—known in their country of origin?
- Who in the Hispanic household consumes it?
- Do they have brand preferences?
- How do they use it?
- How much do they use?
- How often do they use it?
- How often do they purchase it?
- Where do they buy it?
- How much do they spend? Can consumption be increased?

Attitudes and Values Questions

- What values and attitudes do they hold that may impact category decisions?

Psychographics Questions

- What culturally relevant values and attitudes do they hold about life in the U.S. that may impact category decisions?
- What culturally relevant interests do they have that may impact category decisions?[12]

Direct Translation is "Not" In-Culture

Direct translations of a general market advertising strategy tend to be flawed. Something is missing. Some Spanish-language messages directed at consumers lack "cultural attunement," with which Hispanic people can identify. It is akin to showing non-Asians eating their meals with chopsticks. As a consequence, the Spanish-language campaigns may not be reaching as many consumers and are not as effective as they could be. The Spanish-language syntax used in the ads may be correct, but the images, symbols, and context may be wrong or are not in-culture. Consumer research shows that the use of Spanish language is essential to reach this growing share of the U.S. market, but language alone is not the only key to gaining Hispanic customers.

In terms of social interactions from a verbal and non-verbal communications perspective, advertising strategy must also be aligned in-culture. You may have noticed, for example, differences in how we Latinos greet each other and how Anglo Americans greet each other. Americans have a tendency to be informal verbally but physically distant, reserved in their initial contacts and relationships in general. "Typical" Hispanics, on the other hand, tend to be more formal verbally but closer physically in their greetings. The very traditional approach—on first encounters—is to address people by their last names, e.g., "Señor y Señora Gutierrez" (Mr. and Mrs. Gutierrez).

Similarly, in relationships, Hispanics tend to share more about their personal lives, and more often talk about their family, children, and husbands, whereas Anglos tend to be reserved regarding their personal lives.

Having said that, it must be noted that the formal versus informal social orientation varies within the U.S. Hispanic market as well. For example, Caribbean Latinos (Puerto Ricans, Cubans) tend to be more informal than Mexicans and Central/South Americans, particularly the younger generations.

There are also linguistic and grammatical differences that impact how Latinos communicate. The English pronoun "you," for example, is neutral with respect to familiarity and social position. It can be used to address a friend, a child, or the president of the United States. Such neutrality is absent from the Spanish language, where the pronoun "tu" conveys informality and the pronoun "usted" is formal and suggests respect and distance. It would be unthinkable for Hispanics to make use of "el tuteo," the act of using "tu," when addressing a public figure, or in a formal business relationship. The exception is Latinos from Colombia, who use "tu" and "usted" differently, sometimes reversing the formal with the informal pronoun use.

Presently, younger and more acculturated Latinos tend to favor using "tu" in all social interactions. For example, Generation Ñ and New Latinas rarely use "usted," particularly if they are of Caribbean origin. Deciding when to use "tu" or "usted" in marketing communications is not simple and needs to be addressed on a case-by-case basis.

In summary, historically, Hispanic marketing and communications have concentrated on either language or culture, (see Figure 5.13) and only indirectly on "emotions." Emotions were certainly present in the *Share of Heart* philosophy and the in-culture approach also touched on them, but not as the core of the marketing strategy, or the messages' conceptual development. What I observe today is greater focus on positive customer emotions, not only in the U.S. but also abroad; corporate presence in the community, with scholarships, with grants to develop educational programs at universities, or strategically joining forces with NGO or non-for-profit organizations to promote or support health concerns. The link of the brand to "compassion," "caring," "respect," and "positive intent" is visible in the marketplace around the world. It is the positive experience, the good, personalized, and respectful service delivery that is making the difference when selecting the hospital, restaurant, the bank, or the media program. In-culture, "attuned," positive, respectful, and holistic emotions may be the force behind the new successful marketing campaigns to Hispanics. Positive psychology coupled with deep knowledge and understanding of the culture of the target consumer

Emotions = Energy in Motion has the potential to be the next big thing in successful marketing communications and advertising , one-on-one, via electronic media, local or national, via mass media, or all of the above, globally!

Notes

[1] Raheem, Aminah. 1987, 1991, 2000.

[2] Ibid.

[3] Ibid.

[4] M. Isabel Valdés, 2007.

[5] Adapted from Hamburg, 1975.

[6] McGuill, 1983.

[7] Gordon, 1964. Teske and Nelson, as cited in Falicov and Karrer, 1986.

[8] Falcon, 1972.

[9] COSSMHO, 1998.

[10] Falcon, 1972.

[11] Adopted from Theodorson and Theodorson, 1970.

[12] Soto, Terry J. *Marketing to Hispanics: A Strategic Approach to Assessing and Planning Your Initiative.* Kaplan Publishing, 2006.

CHAPTER 6

Share of Heart: The Philosophy

In the mid-1980s, two talented Latino advertisers, Hector and Norma Orci, founders of La Agencia de Orci y Asociados in Los Angeles, developed a Hispanic marketing concept: "to sell me is to know me" and pioneered "emotional marketing." I asked Norma Orci—the brain and heart behind this concept—to describe for this book her now famous philosophy, Share of Heart®. She kindly prepared the following description:

SHARE OF HEART

• Co-founder,
Chief Creative
Officer, La
Agencia de Orci
y Asociados,
3/28/07

by Norma Orci •

Share of Heart is the creative philosophy of our agency, which we developed in the early days to help clients understand why advertising to Latinos needed to be different than advertising to the general market. Share of Heart helped us to articulate the value that Latinos place on relationships, the important part that emotions play in brand selection, and how brands can earn the enduring loyalty of the Latino consumer.

- To build Share of Heart, the advertising needs to:
- Establish rapport by using the language of the consumer
- Provide the information the target needs about the brand
- Offer the most meaningful benefit that the brand can deliver to this consumer
- Present this promise in the most compelling and memorable way
- Wrap it up in production values that are at least as good as those of the general market campaign.

Beyond these basic concepts, Share of Heart advertising demonstrates a deep understanding of how Latinos live, and keen insights into what is important to them. It shows how the brand fits into the world of Latino consumers, and how it can contribute to improving their lives. It reflects Latinos in an attractive and realistic way. Importantly, the advertising and other marketing efforts communicate the manufacturer's genuine regard for Latinos and the Latino community.

The moment Latino consumers experience the brand and confirm that it delivers on all its promises, the brand begins to gain Share of Heart. This relationship will build over time with a consistent message and regular and repeated brand/consumer contact through advertising, promotions and sponsorships, at the point-of-sale and at community events . . . and every time Latinos use the product and are pleased with the results.

The following case study, American Honda, planned and executed by La Agencia de Orci since 1989, illustrates how the Orci's philosophy is applied, and how it still reaps the benefits of the Share of Heart and In-Culture Approach.

CASESTUDY	AMERICAN HONDA

Sixteen years after its pioneering U.S. Hispanic launch, Honda continues to be firmly established as a top brand for American Hispanics.

"This is an example of the benefit to our client of doing it first and doing it right from the very beginning, " said Hector Orci, CEO of La Agencia de Orci y Asociados.

Campaign

Capturing and Retaining the Leadership Position

Background

In 1989 American Honda made a commitment to develop a program

to market automobiles to the U.S. Hispanic market. The first step was to conduct a nationwide search for a Hispanic agency. Later that year, Honda picked La Agencia de Orci & Asociados in Los Angeles.

Honda's first challenge to La Agencia was to "earn the right to sell to Hispanics." Consequently, we spent the first several months in research and developing programs that would introduce Honda to the Hispanic market in a meaningful and long-term way.

Research

The 1989 Hispanic Honda owner was not a typical Hispanic. Before having a Hispanic program in place, Honda had been missing the bulk of the Hispanic new-car buyers, as evidenced in the profiles below.

Figure 6.1

1989 Hispanic Honda Owner	1989 Hispanic New-Car Buyer
Born in the U.S.	Born outside U.S.
Bilingual	Spanish dominant
Avg. HH Income $43,000	Avg. HH Income, $32,000
Single	Married
<2 Children	2+ Children
Professional	Non-professionals
College, Some Post Grad	High School, some College

Honda's Hispanic research also identified problems and opportunities.

| CASESTUDY | AMERICAN HONDA (CONT.) |

The Problems

There was low awareness of Honda among Hispanics. Though slowly gaining acceptance, imports were still perceived as undesirable. Hispanic consumers thought of them as:

- Not elegant
- Small
- Underpowered
- Expensive to repair
- Basically inappropriate for the Hispanic family

The Opportunity

Hispanics who actually owned Hondas loved them and saw them as:

- Roomy
- Powerful
- Elegant
- Ideal for Hispanic families

Research further confirmed that Hispanics wanted to be invited to buy and to see themselves reflected in the advertising. Additionally, Hispanics wanted to see ads for the models they hoped to own: the top-of-the-line models, with all the features, luxury and elegance they aspired to.

Objectives

To implement a dedicated program designed to:

- Earn the right to sell to Hispanics

- Build a long-term relationship with the consumer
- Increase sales to Hispanics
- Provide sales growth opportunities for local dealers

Strategy

We designed a 4-point strategy to build a long-term relationship with Hispanic consumers as detailed below:

- Cultural enrichment

CASESTUDY   AMERICAN HONDA (CONT.)

- Community support
- Sports & entertainment
- Product advertising

Cultural Enrichment

To celebrate the cultural gems that Latin America has contributed to this country, Honda became the founding sponsor of the Ballet Folkolorico de Mexico's U.S. Tour. Since 1989, the annual 20-city tour has been deepening Honda's relationship with the Hispanic community.

The support includes:

- TV ads in the top Hispanic markets
- Radio/TV promotions and giveaways
- Signage at the venue
- Program ad
- Print ads

Community Support

It was important for Honda to demonstrate its interest in and support of issues to the Hispanic community.

It was feared the Hispanic community would not fully participate in the Census, resulting in a significant population undercount. Participation was essential to get a fair share of federal support in the form of schools, hospitals, recreational facilities, and political representation.

With this in mind, the Mexican American Legal Defense and Educational Fund (MALDEF) came to Honda for support. Honda then set out to explain the benefits to Latinos of their

being counted accurately in the 1990 Census. As a result, Honda was recognized as a major contributor in generating the highest level of Hispanic participation in the 1990 Census, which led to increased representation of Hispanics in local and national government.

Sports and Entertainment Sponsorships

In order to win the hearts of Hispanic consumers, Honda began by supporting their favorite sports and entertainment. And by utilizing first-rate media vehicles, Honda strengthened its quality image.

CASESTUDY   AMERICAN HONDA (CONT.)

Sports

Sponsoring major soccer events demonstrated Honda's knowledge of the consumer, and helped to deepen its rapport with the Hispanic community.

In addition, innovative soccer crawls developed for Honda's sponsorship of the 1990 World Cup had great appeal for the target audience and have changed the way the advertising industry now approaches crawl advertising.

- World Cup Soccer Sponsor
    - Italia 1990
    - United States 1994
    - France 1998
- Honda Player of the Year Award: created in 1991, the Honda Award has become the most coveted award in U.S. professional soccer
- Major League Soccer: 1996-1999 exclusive automotive sponsor
- Official sponsor of San Jose Clash team

Entertainment

From 1990 to 1999, Honda reached 1.1 million Hispanic homes each week through *Sabado Gigante,* the longest-running and highest-rated weekly show on Spanish language television.

- National sponsorship of *Sabado Gigante* since 1990
- TV advertising
- Product integration
- Weekly opportunity to win a new Honda
- A visible forum to support Honda's community involvement activities

Product Advertising

Product advertising began in 1990, a full year after initiating activities on the strategic points described above. The advertising was designed to appeal to specific Hispanic needs and to establish a relevant and aspirational image for each Honda model.

Over the years, we have added models to the Hispanic line-up, and have refined product positionings for each model to enhance its appeal to specific target segments. In 1999, they were as follows:

CASESTUDY AMERICAN HONDA (CONT.)

Civic Coupe

Target: Up and coming young Hispanics

Positioning: "The perfect car for all your adventures."

Civic Sedan

Target: Young Hispanic families

Positioning: "Excitement and style in a family sedan."

Accord Sedan

Target: Mature, more affluent adults

Positioning: "Rewards your success and accomplishments."

Odyssey Mini-Van

Target: Established Hispanic families with 2+ kids

Positioning: "A pleasurable family experience."

Results

The results of our Hispanic program are enviable. Not only is Honda the number-one-selling passenger car brand, the Civic and the Accord are the top two-selling car models in the Hispanic market, according to R.L. Polk. In fact, in 1990, the Accord reached the number one position in sales to Hispanics, after only one year of product advertising.

Figure 6.2

Honda U.S. Hispanic Sales Improvement, 2003–2006

2003	2004	2005	2006
+4%	+7%	+8%	+7%

Further, our research tells us that in addition to being a sales success, we have built and nurtured a solid brand with a loyal consumer franchise.

Maintain Honda's leadership positions in awareness and purchase consideration among US Hispanics

Contribute to long-term sales growth objectives

| CASESTUDY | AMERICAN HONDA (CONT.) |

THE 2007 CASE UPDATE

Campaign

Maintain Honda's leadership positions in awareness and purchase consideration among US Hispanics

Contribute to long term sales growth objectives

Strategy

Focus on sales volume leading models

Revamp media mix to include new media/interactive

Combination of product advertising and sponsorship programs

Models Supported

Civic, Accord and introduction of Ridgeline (Honda's first truck)

Media Mix

TV, Radio, Print, Interactive, OOH

Sponsorships

Soccer (MLS, Chivas USA, Honda Player of the Year)

Product Advertising

Civic Sedan

Target: young Hispanic males

Positioning: "Live your best moment."

Accord Sedan

Target: HA 25–54

Positioning: "Quality and reliability with style and performance."

Ridgeline

Target: Hispanic males 35–45

Positioning: "The truck built for strong yet reasonable men."

| CASESTUDY | AMERICAN HONDA (CONT.) |

Results

Honda US Hispanic sales have grown 28% over the past 5 years

2003	+4%
2004	+7%
2005	+8%
2006	+7%

Our Honda client has authorized the release of the information above. As you can see, Honda, 16 years after its pioneering U.S. Hispanic launch, continues to be firmly established as a top brand for American Hispanics. This is an example of the benefit to our client of doing it first and doing it right from the very beginning

—HECTOR ORCI

CHAPTER 7

Revisiting the In-Language Approach

From the 1970s through the 1990s we had to build the case that the Latino market needed to be targeted in Spanish. In the mid-1990s, we recognized the slow emergence of the English-dominant Latino segment, and we brought to the attention of the trade the need to incorporate this segment into their Hispanic marketing plans. Today we have come full-circle, and we need to advocate the relevance of Spanish-language advertising and communications as some marketing managers think they can speak to all Latinos in English! Not the case, as described in earlier chapters. Spanish is not only the primary and emotionally relevant language of large segments of the Hispanic market, but also it touches the "identity" and ethnic identification issues for the majority of U.S. Hispanics today making Spanish a highly effective communications tool to engage Latino customers in-culture!

How to decide? My recommendation is to make language usage decisions based on *hard data*. Even if a growing percentage of Latinos are proficient in English, Spanish continues to be the language of preference for the majority of Hispanic households. Your product or service business strategy, and Latino target should drive the language selection, rather than basing this on what is fashionable or gets more press. Marketing research with the selected target Hispanic segment is highly recommended the right language-use strategy and media mix.

Spanish Language is Here to Stay—For Now!

The ongoing flow of Latino immigrants will continue to replenish the Spanish-dominant consumer pool. Further, as more and more accept the phenomenon of cultural relevance and content driving Latino media behavior, the tenet that Spanish is here to stay for the long run is substantiated. For example, a Latino consumer may read and speak in English very well. Yet if English-language media contents are not relevant, if they don't "talk to" the Latino consumers, they will naturally gravitate towards programs and information sources that connect deeply with them. Chances are that for a large segment of the "traditional" Latino consumer market, the preferred media sources will be in Spanish. Media use shows this clearly. Their preferences can be observed in the programs Latinos across age cohorts choose to watch on Spanish-language television (Figure 7.1) and/or English.

FIGURE 7.1 . . ..

10 Most Popular TV Shows by Total Hispanic Market and Total U.S., 2006–2007
all ages

TOTAL U.S.	TOTAL HISPANIC MARKET
1. American Idol (FOX)	1. Fea Mas Bella (UNI)
2. FOX NFL Sunday (FOX)	2. Barrera de Amor (UNI)
3. Dancing with the Stars (ABC)	3. Duelo de Passiones (UNI)
4. CSI (CBS)	4. Mundo de Fieras (UNI)
5. CBS NFL National (CBS)	5. Heridas de Amor (UNI)
6. Grey's Anatomy (ABC)	6. Bailando Boda Suenos (UNI)
7. Desperate Housewives (ABC)	7. Christina (UNI)
8. House (FOX)	8. Don Francisco Presenta (UNI)
9. NBC Sunday Night Football (NBC)	9. Aqui y Ahora (UNI)
10. CSI: Miami (CBS)	10. Casos Vida R: Ed. ESP (UNI)

Source: Nielsen Media Research. NHTI, 09/18/2006-02/25/2007, M-Su 6a-6a (excludes breakouts and specials).

In 2007, the ten most popular programs watched by the Hispanic market, according to Nielsen Media Research, are all in Spanish and presented via Spanish-language television. The only age segment for whom this is not entirely the case is the 12-to-17-year-olds (Figure 7.2), in which only half of the top ten programs watched are in Spanish, and the rest are in English. However, the top four programs are still in Spanish.

FIGURE 7.2 . . . .

10 Most Popular TV Shows by Total Hispanic Market and Total U.S., 2006–2007
aged 12 to 17

TOTAL U.S.	TOTAL HISPANIC MARKET
1. American Idol (FOX)	1. Fea Mas Bella (UNI)
2. Family Guy (FOX)	2. Barrera de Amor (UNI)
3. House (FOX)	3. Mundo de Fieras (UNI)
4. The Simpsons (FOX)	4. Bailando Boda Suenos (UNI)
5. Desperate Housewives (ABC)	5. Family Guy (FOX)
6. American Dad (FOX)	6. Heridas de Amor (UNI)
7. Heroes (NBC)	7. Friday Night Smackdown (CW)
8. FOX NFL Sunday (FOX)	8. American Idol (FOX)
9. Lost (ABC)	9. American Dad (FOX)
10. Grey's Anatomy (ABC)	10. The Simpsons (FOX)

Source: Nielsen Media Research. NHTI, 09/18/2006-02/25/2007, M-Su 6a-6a (excludes breakouts and specials).

This media use behavior suggests that even if English proficiency continues to increase dramatically in the coming years, Spanish-language usage and media will most likely continue to be highly popular among Hispanics in the U.S.

Managing the Language Puzzle

Language media selection is the most complex and fascinating piece of the Hispanic marketing mix and strategy, not only because of its communication power, but also because it is the "vehicle" of our emotions, needs and wants, memories, and knowledge. It is the only means by which to bridge the separation between you and me to become "us," yet it can also be the most powerful means for negativity.

My personal experience vis-à-vis language acquisition and usage tells a story that may shed light into the immigrant language-usage puzzle. I grew up on three different continents and my languages became useful when developing marketing and advertising strategies. For example, since the first language I learned as a toddler was German—Deutsch—I can easily relive my early childhood memories and experiences when I hear German, like an instantaneous jump back in time. Listening to German songs of that period is even more effective.

FIGURE 7.3 . . . .

English Ability by Age, 2006

foreign-Born, U.S.-born (2nd and 3rd+) generations

	UNDER 18			18 AND OVER		
	ENGLISH ONLY	ENGLISH VERY WELL	ENGLISH LESS THAN VERY WELL	ENGLISH ONLY	ENGLISH VERY WELL	ENGLISH LESS THAN VERY WELL
Hispanic	30.9	49.5	19.5	18.3	35.1	46.6
U.S. Born	35.9	49.3	14.8	35.9	49.8	14.3
Foreign Born	3.3	50.6	46.1	4.0	23.2	72.9
Total U.S. Population	80.0	14.6	5.4	80.7	9.8	9.5

Source: Pew Hispanic Center tabulations of 2005 American Community Survey.

During my formative years growing up in Chile, I learned Spanish, which would become the primary language I spoke as a teenager and young adult—when I first experienced love and loss.

However, most of my professional skills were acquired in the U.S. and as a result, even though I know most of the same professional vocabulary in Spanish, it is sometimes challenging to communicate for work in Spanish. A more simple example: I can add, subtract, and recite multiplication tables and the alphabet easiest in Spanish. I also react quickest in Spanish, not English. The connotations and denotations of the words are similar in both languages, yet knowledge of the same words is not enough; something is missing.

In other words, language carries not only the meanings (connotations and denotations) of each word, but also the circumstances, or lifestage in which these were often used, the emotional vibes and experiences these words "lived" with us—what they meant at that particular time! For instance, a street we grew up walking every day to school evokes different memories and emotions than the streets we "rush" through when we go to work. The emotional connections with the street are so different, from the details we remember, so much deeper and richer for those we walked during our childhood or formative days as compared with those we presently drive. Now, we have no time to focus, observe, and memorize, enjoy the beauty and pleasure of the seasons as these change, the scents, the nice or ugly buildings. We probably just remember how many traffic lights they have and how fast they turn to green. The words I learned with "quality time" are far richer and profound in meanings than those I learned with stress, pressure, and "self-consciousness!" No wonder they say that for those who communicate in more than one language on a daily basis, the first language connects us deeper with our emotions!

"Pardon Me, Do You Speak English?" (Crispell, 1992) was the title of an article in *American Demographics* reporting data on a growing American phenomenon of "linguistically isolated households," the term the 1990 U.S. Census used to refer to households in which no one older than 16 could communicate in English (well enough to communicate with English-speaking people). These households tend to be isolated from mainstream American culture and, to a large extent, unreachable via traditional English-language media, marketing, and advertising strategies.

Most community based vendors talk to their customers in Spanish. Catholic churches, representing the dominant religion for Hispanics, reach their congregations through services conducted in Spanish. Shops and supermarkets satisfy consumers' longing for traditional Hispanic foods, clothing, and amenities along with their newly acquired tastes for American products. Given the share of immigration from Latin America to the United States and Hispanic immigration projections into the future, Spanish will continue to be a popular language in the United States, and it will undoubtedly be an effective tool for marketing to Hispanics—particularly adults.

Language Usage and Preferences

Of all social traits, language is perhaps the most distinguishable characteristic of any culture and probably the last one any immigrant group will relinquish. As has been documented extensively, given the choice, most foreign-born Latinos choose to speak Spanish rather than English, and some second and third generation Latinos speak Spanish well, depending on the market, the place where they grew up, and their bond with their culture and country of origin.

Spanish use and proficiency does decrease with generational distance. However, many do keep the language of their culture alive. Spanish language carries a strong emotional bond with "being Latino." In these times of turbulence, due to the immigration debate, allegiance to Hispanic culture and language grows.

Studies show that U.S.-born Millennials and young Latinos are more likely to speak Spanish fluently "if the parents spoke the language at home and

enforced it." However, this is not always the case, and the language of preference for many youths is English. Presently, 38.5 percent of Hispanic households
in which English is spoken "very well" say they do not speak English at home
(see Figure 7.4). If the 38.7 percent of households that only speak Spanish—at
home and away from home—are added, 77.2 percent of the families are in fact
making the future of the Spanish language in the U.S. a certain fact.

"When," "why," and "with whom" Latinos use or do not use Spanish depends
on several factors, and sadly for marketers and advertisers, this is not a simple
black-and-white issue.

It requires deep knowledge of the targeted segment. For example, bilingual
Latinos may choose to communicate in Spanish in some contexts, such as fam-
ily gatherings, and when reading books and local newspapers (if available in
Spanish). Federico Subervi and et al (*Handbook of Hispanic Cultures of the United
States*, Arte Publico Press, 1994) refers to this as "Situational Latinidad."

As suggested earlier, it is highly possible that Spanish-language use will
continue to play a major role in the Hispanic market in the foreseeable future
if current immigration projections hold and families continue to communicate
in Spanish at home, however, as mentioned earlier, the younger generations
are acculturating faster and using English language more often than previous
generations.

FIGURE 7.4 . . . .

Language Spoken at Home and English-Speaking Ability, 2004
aged 5 and older

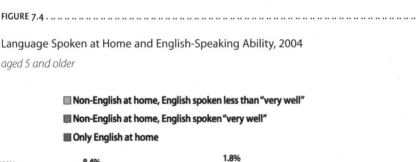

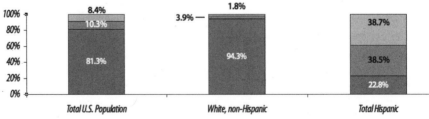

*Data based on sample limited to the household population and exclude the population living in institutions, college
dormitories, and other group quarters. For information on confidentiality protection, sampling error, nonsampling error,
and definitions, see factfinder.census.gov/home/en/datanotes/exp_acs2004.html*

Source: U.S. Census Bureau, 2004 American Community Survey, Selected Population Profiles, S0201.

There is considerable variation regarding language proficiency depending on the country of origin, as shown in Figure 7.5. The largest cultural segment in the market, the Mexican population that represents over two-thirds of the Hispanic market, has the second largest Spanish-only household segments, similar to the non-Mexican Central American.

This supports the suggestion that Spanish is at the present time a dominant language for marketing to Mexicans and Central Americans, since it is possible that the youngsters in these households are not yet making the purchase decisions—except in those categories that affect them directly, such as music, iPods, cell phones, movies and CDs, and sports gear; if over age 16 (in some states), gas and after car products may also be included.

FIGURE 7.5 . . . .

Hispanic Language Spoken at Home and English-Speaking Ability

aged 5 and older by country of origin, 2004

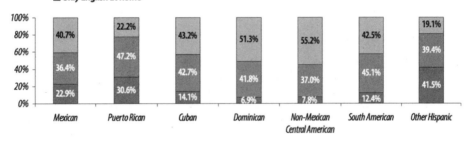

Data based on sample limited to the household population and exclude the population living in institutions, college dormitories, and other group quarters. For information on confidentiality protection, sampling error, nonsampling error, and definitions, see factfinder.census.gov/home/en/datanotes/exp_acs2004.html

Source: U.S. Census Bureau, 2004 American Community Survey, Selected Population Profiles, S0201.

Language Segmentation: A "Proxy" for Acculturation

Many consumer studies indicate that adult consumers' preference for the Spanish language is perhaps the strongest indicator of Hispanic culture. After conducting numerous studies and interviews among Hispanic adults, we developed the Hispanic Language-based Segmentation at Hispanic Market Connection, a rating scale based on a battery of questions concerning usage and proficiency in Spanish and English. Based on scales regarding proficiency in English and Spanish (speaking and reading abilities) and media usage patterns in both or either language, we identified five language-based segments:

- Spanish-only

- Spanish-preferred

- True bilinguals

- English-preferred

- English-only

These language-based segments divide consumers into distinct "marketing" groups or cohorts. They are based on self-reported levels of proficiency in English and Spanish. The five segments are defined as follows:

Spanish-only or Monolingual. The consumer depends on Spanish to communicate and has limited or no command of English. He or she is foreign-born and is usually an adult who is a recent arrival. In many cases, but not always, he or she is of lower socioeconomic status as well.

Spanish-preferred. Spanish-language skills are considerably better than English-language skills. The consumer knows enough English to get around; however, he or she feels more comfortable communicating in Spanish. The majority in this segment are foreign-born, and have resided for several years in the U.S. Their socioeconomic status improves considerably in proportion to the number of years living in the United States.

Bilingual. They are able to communicate freely in either Spanish or English. Consumers in this segment can be either foreign-born or U.S.-born. Most grew up exposed to both cultures, either at home or in their neighborhoods. Their socioeconomic status improves dramatically.

English-preferred. English-language skills of these consumers are considerably better than Spanish-language skills. They know just enough Spanish to get around, but prefer and are more comfortable communicating in English. Most people in this segment are U.S.-born or went to grade school in the United States and have been exposed to both Hispanic and Anglo-American cultures.

English-only. This monolingual consumer communicates only in English, has little or no command of Spanish, and tends to have higher socioeconomic status and greater exposure to Anglo-American culture, lifestyle, and values.

Even though language-based segmentations do not address directly the acculturation level of the consumers, they are directionally correct and can be used as a "proxy" to ascertain where they are located in the acculturation continuum.

Language Segments by DMAs

Different cities have distinct profiles of language usage that should be considered when planning a national Hispanic marketing initiative in-culture.

Historically, cities with a greater influx of new Latino immigrants tend to have larger Spanish-dominant/Spanish-preferred consumers. Miami, Dallas/Ft. Worth, and Los Angeles are good examples. Similarly, cities with low immigration tend to have larger percentages of English-dominant Latinos; for example San Antonio and Phoenix. Latin Force (formerly Geoscape) a geo-segmentation services company, creates language-based segments for the ten largest Hispanic DMA's based on several Hispanic population data sources and their own studies. The granularity of Geoscape's segmentation allows for a very detailed picture of the language distribution in these DMAs. (Figure 7.6)

FIGURE 7.6 . . . .

Language Usage in the 10 Largest Hispanic DMA's, 2007

5 years of age and older

	ENGLISH DOMINANT	BILINGUAL: ENGLISH PREFERRED	BILINGUAL: EQUAL SPANISH AND ENGLISH	BILINGUAL: SPANISH PREFERRED	SPANISH DOMINANT
Los Angeles	16.9%	24.8%	14.4%	21.5%	22.3%
New York	12.2	26.9	16.5	22.9	21.6
Miami / Ft. Lauderdale	5.9	26.9	16.6	23.1	27.5
Houston	14.6	26.0	16.0	20.5	22.9
Chicago	14.4	24.2	15.6	22.8	23.1
Dallas / Ft. Worth	15.7	23.4	13.9	20.8	26.2
San Francisco / San Jose	23.5	24.7	13.3	19.0	19.4
Phoenix (Prescott)	24.9	25.0	13.6	16.7	19.8
San Antonio	24.5	37.4	14.7	12.7	10.7
Harlingen / Weslaco / Brownsville / McAllen	7.0	29.8	21.6	21.5	20.1

Source: Latin Force data estimates, 2007.

A visual representation of the ten top Hispanic DMAs by language seg-ments "tells the true story" of language proficiency and levels of acculturation differences in these DMAs. (Figure 7.7)

FIGURE 7.7 . . . .

Language Usage

5 years of age and older

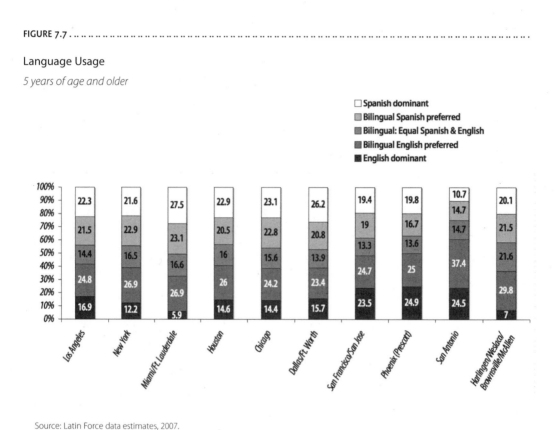

Source: Latin Force data estimates, 2007.

As is the case with most statistics, it is easy to manipulate the data to "tell a different story." In Figure 7.8 below, we have aggregated some of the language segments in each DMA, grouping "all those segments that speak at least some English"; that is, the "Bilingual: Spanish-Preferred," "Bilingual: Equal Spanish and English," and "Bilingual: English-Preferred." These three segments include consumers with very different degrees of proficiency in English, and therefore, acculturation levels. In-culture messages to each group should probably be quite different to be emotionally engaging, moving, and enticing. However, the data is veridical, and somebody could say that the vast majority of the U.S. Latino population communicates in English!

FIGURE 7.8 . . . .

Language Usage in the 10 Largest Hispanic DMAs, 2007

5 years of age and older

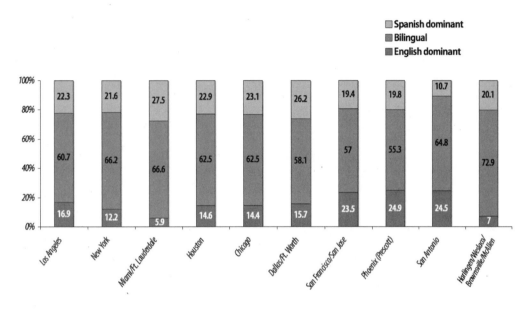

Source: Latin Force data estimates, 2007.

Similarly, Figure 7.9, using the same set of data, has been aggregated in a different set of segments; the Latino consumers that are predominantly fluent in each language; "Spanish Dominant/Preferred" are a large language segment in each DMA; similarly, those Latinos who are "English Dominant/Preferred," are a second large language segment in these DMA's.

Why is this exercise important? Because you need to be aware that the language preference issue can be presented in quite a different light, depending on what position wants to be advanced; e.g. "The vast majority of the Hispanic population speaks English," as the first case shows, or the opposite case, "Over a third of Latinos in all DMA's speak Spanish." If we were to add the "Bilingual" segment to the Spanish-speaking group, this would be the largest language segment in most DMA's. It all depends on who you want to sell what! And they are all true.

Language Usage in the 10 Largest Hispanic DMAs, 2007

5 years of age and older

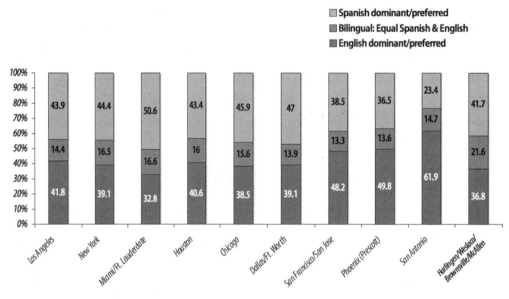

Source: Latin Force data estimates, 2007.

Language and Media Use

Most Hispanics use both English and Spanish media. The frequency with which they choose one or the other, however, varies drastically depending on age and language proficiency.

As would be expected, the fewer the number of years that Hispanic adults have lived in the United States, the lower their English proficiency and the greater their use of Spanish-language media are. This rule, however, does not apply across the board. Many long-term U.S. residents and also some second-generation Hispanics, both highly English proficient, consume some Spanish-language media.

This behavior is "content driven." If the internet has interesting Spanish language websites—or information not available in English language websites—these Latino consumers will visit the Spanish sites.

The same is true with all media sources. If the news in Spanish covers Latin American news or sports events in South America, or other information not included in English-language media, these bilingual Latinos will watch, listen to, or read Spanish-language media. Conversely, more and more young Latino adults and teens prefer English-language media consistent with their acculturation levels and lifestyles, even if they have resided in the United States for only a few years. Latino teens, like most teenagers, want to be like their peers and participate fully in the activities of their peer group. Media is not an exception. Hence, as the new Latino Millennials and children grow up, English-language media will be positioned to own the largest share of the media audience in the Hispanic market. This may vary of course if the emerging bilingual Latino prefers Spanish-language media and the existing media outlets find a way to appeal to this young audience.

FIGURE 7.10 .. ..

Hispanic Media Consumption by Language and Generation , 2002

LANGUAGE PREFERENCE	ALL HISPANICS	U.S.- BORN	1ST GENERATION/ FOREIGN-BORN
Predominantly Spanish	38%	9%	55%
Spanish and English Equally	26%	20%	30%
Predominantly English	36%	71%	15%

Source: Pew Hispanic Center, 2002 National Hispanic Survey in the U.S.

Again, it stands to reason that Spanish should be the language selected to advertise to the majority of the Hispanic adults today for such products as home improvement, food, insurance and other financial products, travel, entertainment, cars, restaurants, over-the-counter medicines, and healthcare services.

English-language media play the same informational role to true bilinguals and English-preferred consumers as to the general market. Spanish and English-language media complement each other in Hispanic marketing communication strategies, but our research has shown that acculturated Hispanics tend to respond better to advertising that is culturally attuned, even if the message itself is delivered in English.

CHAPTER 8

The GenAge Paradigm

Acculturation is an ongoing process, a continuum with blurred boundaries; it is impossible to say with certainty if a consumer is 10 percent, 30 percent, or 50 percent acculturated. What we do know is that acculturation does happen, that it is a complex, uneven process, and that marketers need to work with approximations to successfully manage acculturating populations. We also know acculturation will continue to challenge the best Hispanic marketers and advertising strategists for the foreseeable future.

The GenAge Segments

Based on Hispanic age and generational data gathered by the U.S. Census Bureau, and with the help of demographers, we developed a new version of the Hispanic age-based segmentation and revamped it to be more practical and "user-friendly." Each GenAge segment shows the percentage of foreign-born and U.S.-born, and a generational breakdown to bring to the marketer's attention an approximate picture of what the acculturation mindset of the particular age segments might be. For example, if the majority of a GenAge segment is foreign-born, chances are they did not grow up in the U.S. since only an estimated 5 to 8 percent of foreign-born Hispanics immigrate as children. Consumers in this foreign-born segment may be at various points on the acculturation continuum, but for most of them, chances are Spanish is their first, and most effective, emotional language.

Five Core Age Segments and Nine Sub-Segments

Five core segments were created based on the natural breaks of the U.S. Hispanic population distribution and the marketing value they represent. In addition, *in-culture* criteria were used, following the "traditional Latino life cycle" and cultural mindset, as described earlier in this book.

FIGURE 8.1 . . . .

Five Core Age Segments

0 to 9	Los Bebès/Los Niños
10 to 19	Generation Ñ
20 to 39	Latinos/Latinas
40 to 59	Los Boomers
60+	Los Grandes

The five main segments are sub-divided to create nine finer segments that more closely reflect the different lifecycle points in a consumer's life. With the exception of the "Los Grandes" segment whose population size is presently too small to be subdivided, the core age segments are too broad and hence not valuable for certain marketing applications. For example, there are significant differences in the life stages of a 25-year-old and a 35-year-old consumer with the consequent marketing implications in terms of income, purchase behavior, lifestyle, and so forth.

FIGURE 8.2 . . . .

Nine Age Sub-Segments

0 to 5	Los Bebès
6 to 9	Los Niños
10 to 14	Tweens
15 to 19	Teens
20 to 29	Twenty-somethings
30 to 39	Thirty-somethings
40 to 49	Young Boomers
50 to 59	Mature Boomers
60+	Los Grandes

Figure 8.3 shows the two age segmentation schemes and the percent of the U.S. Hispanic population in each. The outer circle shows the *five core age segments*, and the inner circle shows the *nine age sub-segments*.

FIGURE 8.3 . . . .

The GenAge Segmentation, 2006
Hispanic Age-Based Segments and Sub-Segments

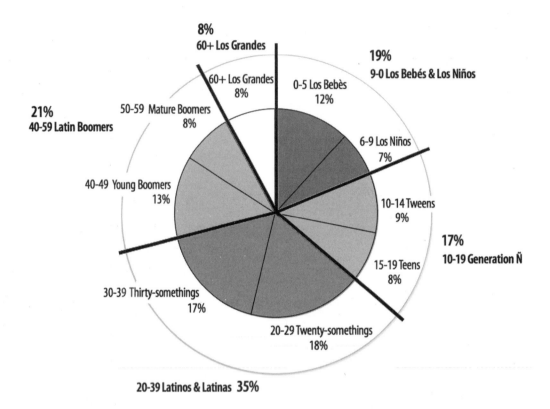

8%
60+ Los Grandes

19%
9-0 Los Bebés & Los Niños

60+ Los Grandes
8%

0-5 Los Bebès
12%

50-59 Mature Boomers
8%

6-9 Los Niños
7%

21%
40-59 Latin Boomers

40-49 Young Boomers
13%

10-14 Tweens
9%

17%
10-19 Generation Ñ

30-39 Thirty-somethings
17%

15-19 Teens
8%

20-29 Twenty-somethings
18%

20-39 Latinos & Latinas 35%

Source: M. Isabel Valdés. The 2006 data is consistent with independent estimates including those from the Pew Hispanic Center and the Census Bureau's 2006 March Current Population Survey, Annual Social and Economic Supplement. ©2007.

The Generation Factor

Because the generation or "G" factor is hugely pervasive and relevant to developing successful Hispanic marketing today, the GenAge Segmentation incorporates generational breaks within each age segment and sub-segment.

First Generation: Foreign-born

Second Generation: U.S.-born of foreign-born parents

Third Generation (and up): Native-born of native-born parents, grandparents, and so on.

Each GenAge segment shows the percentage within each age segment that:

Is foreign-born—First Generation

Was born in the U.S.—Second Generation

Was born to parents already born in the U.S.—Third+ Generation

Figure 8.4 illustrates the size of each segment by age and generational breaks, clearly showing the generational, or G-factor differences for the age groups, and, more importantly, the difference in the size of the segments.

FIGURE 8.4 . . . .

GenAge Segmentation by Nine Age Sub-Segments and Generation, 2006

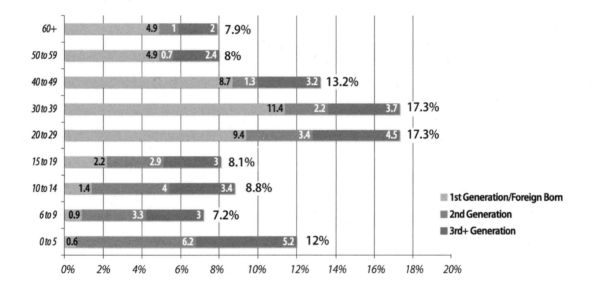

Source: M. Isabel Valdés. 2006 data is consistent with independent estimates including those from the Pew Hispanic Center and the Census Bureau's 2006 March Current Population Survey, Annual Social and Economic Supplement. © 2007

The "sweet spot," or high-value consumer segments targeted by many marketers today are *twenty-somethings* (20–29) and *thirty-somethings* (30–39). These age segments presently dominate the U.S. Hispanic market, each representing 17.3 percent of the population. Many of these are foreign-born, first-generation Latinos.

As presented earlier in the acculturation section (Chapter 4), many of these consumers are bilingual/Spanish-preferred. Depending on the context, they may prefer to communicate in Spanish but they consume English as well as Spanish-language media. They tend to hold traditional Hispanic cultural values, but with "less strength" than their non-acculturated counterparts. They are in the prime family formation years and the women are the primary shoppers.

A smaller, yet significant percentage of these GenAge segments are U.S.-born, second and third generation, and may have completely different lifestyles and cultural value orientation than their foreign-born counterparts.

FIGURE 8.5 . . . .

Hispanic Population Projection by Age Segments, 2005–2050

(in thousands)

	2005	2010	2020	2030	2040	2050
0 to 5	5,209	5,752	6,651	7,782	9,026	10,154
6 to 9	3,080	3,587	4,226	4,873	5,716	6,481
10 to 14	3,853	4,057	5,075	5,845	6,813	7,834
15 to 19	3,576	4,162	4,950	5,779	6,616	7,660
20 to 29	7,385	7,805	9,370	11,298	12,947	14,716
30 to 39	6,964	7,742	8,442	10,106	12,092	13,703
40 to 49	5,301	6,282	7,878	8,630	10,332	12,295
50 to 59	3,216	4,177	6,178	7,765	8,546	10,233
60 to 69	1,723	2,307	3,932	5,814	7,349	8,134
70+	1,495	1,884	3,054	5,164	8,146	11,348
Total	41,802	47,755	59,756	73,056	87,583	102,558

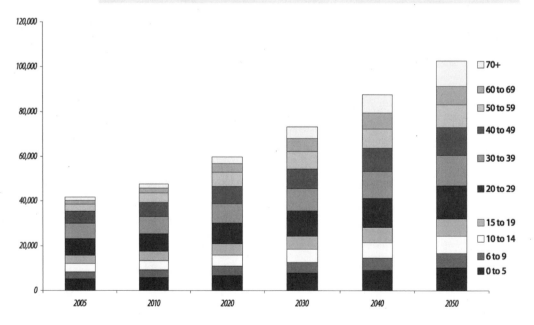

Source: M. Isabel Valdés, 2007, adapted from U.S. Census usproj2000-2050.xls

The Generational Crossover

The demographic shifts taking place in the Hispanic market are enormous. Figure 8.5 illustrates this phenomenon. Impacts of these shifts in the marketplace can be difficult to pinpoint and manage, but they have deep implications in Hispanic marketing.

The demographic and generational "crossover" of the dominant foreign-born or first generation created by the waves of immigrants of the great migration of the 1960s with the second and third+ generations of U.S-born Latinos is important from a marketing standpoint. The desegregation of the U.S.-born Latinos by generation and age in the graph gives us a glimpse of what the Hispanic market will look like in the decades to come, when these young Latinos are full-fledged decision-makers, consumers, voters and workers, and the foreign-born consumers move to the older age segments.

FIGURE 8.6 . . . .

GenAge Segments, 2006

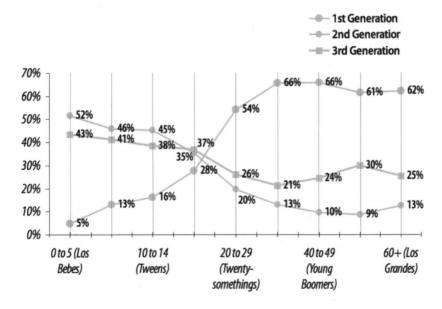

Hispanic Population Median Age 2006: 28
Total U.S. Population Median Age 2006: 35.5

Source: M. Isabel Valdés, The 2007 data is consistent with independent estimates including those from the Pew Hispanic Center and the Census Bureau's 2006 March Current Population Survey, Annual Social and Economic Supplement. © 2007 M. Isabel Valdés

A decade ago, when Latino crossover consumers were just 5-to-9-year-olds, their presence in the overall marketplace was less visible, except of course in the categories related to new-born babies and children. However, as kid's marketing experts show (*The Kid's Market: Myth and Realities.* McNeal, 1999), these young consumers form their brand loyalties early in life, building "emotional connections with brands," acquiring value orientations and preferences, and entering the consumer market much earlier than previous generations. Hence, marketers that are not communicating with young Latinos, directly or through their parents, are missing the opportunity of future brand loyalty. The crossover Latino teens, together with the almost 20 percent of the Latino population in the 20-to-30 age segment are making their preferences heard in the marketplace as trend-setters and consumers, as they enter the labor force and begin having families of their own.

In previous decades, second generation U.S.-born Hispanics represented only 9 to 13 percent of the sweet spot GenAge segments (20-40 years old). Third generations and later had a share 21 percent to 30 percent, but the majority (54 to 66 percent) of shoppers in these age groups were foreign-born. Hence, the main marketing and communications focus was to the foreign-born and in their traditional Hispanic culture and language.

These proportions are changing rapidly as can be seen in Figure 8.6. How soon these U.S.-born Latinos change the culture is yet to be seen. Will we become a "melting pot" as has been anticipated? Or will a mosaic of segments co-exist, each one maintaining its own culture, as Canada has mastered, with great respect and enjoyment in their bilingual, bicultural society? Only time will tell.

Room for Misconceptions

Many second and third generation Latinos are active in the Hispanic community. They have succeeded in leadership roles in politics, corporate America, and as entrepreneurs, creating new businesses and contributing to the arts, health care, religion, finances, philanthropy, etc. Their success and visibility may lead some to believe that the entire Hispanic market today is like them, fully English-speaking or bilingual and acculturated, and can be targeted successfully with little or no Spanish. However, this is not yet the case and thinking this way may lead marketers in the wrong direction!

The danger is in not understanding how the acculturation process progresses (see Chapter 2) and in not recognizing that the non-acculturated Hispanic consumer presence is still huge. Just the large numbers of Latinos watching Spanish-language TV, listening to Spanish-language radio, and reading Spanish-language print media attest to the presence of a very large segment of Spanish-dominant speakers in the market. The fact that many foreign-born Latinos have resided most of their lives in the U.S. does not automatically erase their native language and culture. As traditional Hispanic cultural traits mentioned earlier (such as *Familismo, Machismo, Marianismo, Chicoismo*), are found across generations today, there is a gradual acculturation process that takes place. Concluding that Hispanics are 100 percent acculturated in one generation is simplistic and can cause dangerously misleading conclusions!

Foreign-Born Hispanics as a Target Segment

The majority of Latino shoppers in key age segments—age 29 and up—are foreign-born and are active shoppers, influencers, and decision makers. Even if their English proficiency is much better today than a decade or two ago, they are the same people, born in another country, with different life stories and expectations than those born in the United States. That cannot be changed. As described in greater detail in Chapter 4, and in many other works, just speaking in English and "learning the social ropes" of the U.S. does not necessarily change who we are at the core.

In product and service categories that are not geared towards younger consumers, it is possible that your marketing strategies should be focused on the large foreign-born population, rather than the younger, U.S.-born population for several reasons. First, because the number of new Latino immigrants continues to increase; second, because long-term residents who have resided in the U.S. thirty years or more continue to discover cultural and information gaps as they enter new life-cycle stages; and last, most of the crossover Latino segments, teens and younger, are still young and are children of foreign-born parents who make the purchase decisions in key categories such as financial services, mortgages, insurance, retirement, health insurance, travel, and transportation, as well as what foods will be purchased for home use.

Each GenAge segment will be described in detail in the next chapters and each chapter will provide examples for everyday application of these insights.

FIGURE 8.7 . . . .

Hispanic Age Segmentation Projections, 2005 and 2010

(in thousands)

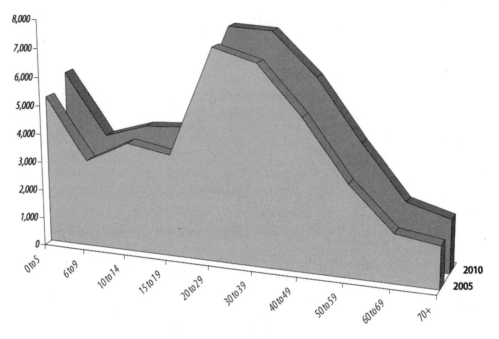

Source: M. Isabel Valdés, 2007, based on U.S. Census 2005 data

In a few years, the crossover generation will be at the threshold of adult-hood. By 2010, the 15-to-19 age segment will be 20-to-24, forming families. Those who went to college will be graduating and the vast majority will be active in the labor force. As consumers, they will reflect the results of advertising and marketing efforts directed at them. Those marketing and communication strategies that have addressed in their messages the typical "gaps" of consumers raised in new immigrant households (that is, children of foreign-born parents), will be positioned in a better place to enjoy longer-term brand loyalty. For example, if a consumer has not grown up enjoying traditional American brands, they will be less likely to develop enduring "emotional bonds" with the brand, or even the category.

FIGURE 8.8 . . . .

GenAge Segments, 2006

age segments by size and percent of the total Hispanic market

5 MAIN SEGMENTS	9 SUB-SEGMENTS	SEGMENT SIZE (IN 000S)	% OF TOTAL U.S. HISPANIC POP.
0 to 9 Los Bebès/Los Niños		8,599	19.2%
	0 to 5 Los Bebès	5,345	12.0%
	6 to 9 Los Niños	3,254	7.2%
10 to 19 Generation Ñ		7,576	17.0%
	10 to 14 Tweens	3,977	8.8%
	15 to 19 Teens	3,599	8.1%
20 to 39 Latinos/Latinas		15,460	34.6%
	20 to 29 Twenty-somethings	7,740	17.3%
	30 to 39 Thirty-somethings	7,720	17.3%
40 to 59 Los Boomers		9,505	21.3%
	40 to 49 Young Boomers	5,927	13.2%
	50 to 59 Mature Boomers	3,578	8.0%
60+ Los Grandes		3,511	7.9%
Total		44,652*	100%

*Does not include Puerto Rico's 3.9 million Hispanics nor Census undercount.

Source: The 2006 data is consistent with independent estimates including those from the Pew Hispanic Center and the Census Bureau's 2006 March Current Population Survey, Annual Social and Economic Supplement.

Marketing to Latinos by Generation

Some marketing strategies call for targeting specific generations. For example, you may want to market a product or service to first generation Latinos who were born in a foreign country and that migrated as adults. As previously mentioned, studies show that the vast majority (95 percent) of Hispanic immigrants arrive after age 18.

Targeting foreign-born Latinos has been common practice the past two decades, since these are "low-hanging fruit" for brand managers eager to win another point in market share, but that is beginning to shift.

Figure 8.9 shows the breakdown of estimated foreign-born Latinos residing in the U.S. today—45 percent, or 19.9 million consumers. The U.S.-born Hispanic segment, including second and third+ generations, is 55 percent, or 24.8 million, and the majority are between the ages of 20 to 59.

Hispanic Population by Generation, 2006

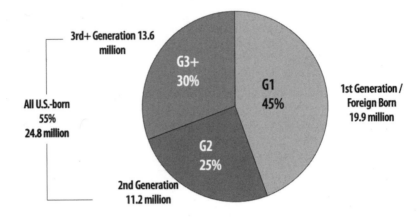

*Does not include Puerto Rico's 3.9 million Hispanics nor Census undercount.

Source: M. Isabel Valdés. The 2006 data is consistent with independent estimates including those from the Pew Hispanic Center and the Census Bureau's 2006 March Current Population Survey, Annual Social and Economic Supplement. © 2007.

GenAge Segments: Foreign-Born/First-Generation

Each of the generations has its own profile that may come in handy when targeting a specific product or service, or even political campaign. Below is a graphic representation of each generation by age.

GenAge Segments: First Generation (Foreign-Born)

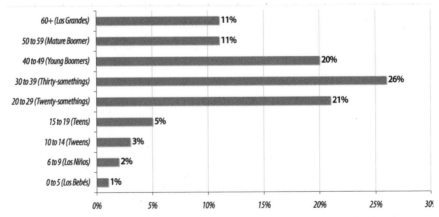

Source: M. Isabel Valdés 2007. The 2006 data is consistent with independent estimates including those from the Pew Hispanic Center and the Census Bureau's 2006 March Current Population Survey, Annual Social and Economic Supplement, © 2007

GenAge Segments: Second Generation

Presently, we may be interested in targeting second generation GenAge segments for youth-oriented products. This makes sense, as the vast majority of the second GenAge segment is under age 20: Los Bebès, Los Niños, Tweens and Teens, and the Twenty-somethings. Bilingual, or English-preferred/dominant, these young consumers may speak mostly English, but culturally speaking "Latino" traditional music, sports, values of family, and group orientation still weigh heavily in their mindset. Hence, it would be a mistake not to target them in-culture.

The second generation population size is 11.2 million

FIGURE 8.11 .. ..

GenAge Segments: Second Generation

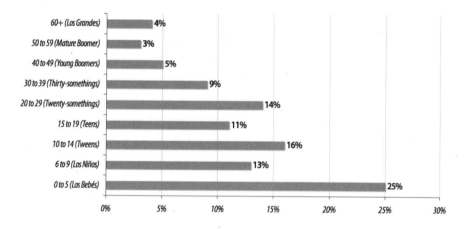

Source: M. Isabel Valdés. The 2006 data is consistent with independent estimates including those from the Pew Hispanic Center and the Census Bureau's 2006 March Current Population Survey, Annual Social and Economic Supplement. © 2007.

GenAge Segments: Third+ Generation

The third+ generation is a growing and attractive GenAge segment, with 13.6 million Latino consumers. Their greater degree of acculturation into the mainstream market calls for a different in-culture marketing strategy. This could certainly be in English; however, some Latino cultural identification will still exist. As the Hispanic market matures, the third generation will continue growing into a relevant role in society and the marketplace.

The questions we need to ask of a particular segment relate to the strength of their Hispanic ethnic affiliation, their acculturation, and their preferences as a community. For example, the African-American market communicates very well in English and was mostly raised in the United States. However, research studies show African Americans have a distinct culture and have strong ethnic affiliation. Hence, they respond significantly better when marketing communications strategies reflect, talk to, and respect their unique culture. Therefore, it is highly possible that future, acculturated Hispanic generations will continue to appreciate being addressed and talked to in a unique, acculturated, in-culture Hispanic language.

FIGURE 8.12 .. ..

GenAge Segments: Third+ Generation

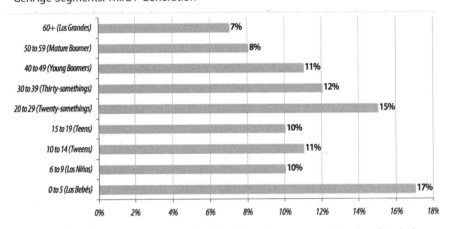

Source: M. Isabel Valdés. The 2006 data is consistent with independent estimates including those from the Pew Hispanic Center and the Census Bureau's 2006 March Current Population Survey, Annual Social and Economic Supplement. © 2007.

The growth and changes taking place at the core of the Hispanic market are unique, never before seen in the history of marketing. The longitudinal migration, now strong for several decades, confronts us with marketing challenges and dynamics that are not found in any marketing textbook.

However, it is imperative to meet those challenges and to do it right. Hispanics are 15 percent share of the U.S. population today, and poised to become 25 percent by 2050. We must become more intelligent Hispanic marketers and go full speed ahead, today.

The growth in Hispanic markets will continue to contribute bottom-line profits if it is approached with deep understanding, going beyond the numbers and learning the culture that underpins the demographic data. This way, your business and marketing plans will be based on comprehensive, real knowledge that you can apply strategically, in-culture, and in-acculturation.

CASESTUDY   CHURCH'S CHICKEN

Campaign: "Truly Spicy"
Agency: Cartel Creativo

Background

Church's chicken is a regional quick service restaurant (QSR) chain that has built its reputation on its authentic fried chicken. Presently, Church's has been playing a competitive game of action and reaction with its key competitors, Kentucky Fried Chicken and Popeyes. The product mix for spicy chicken has declined tremendously in the last year, from 30 percent to 18 percent. In market share, Popeyes is the nearest competitor for providing "spicy" chicken products.

Church's decided to take a bold initiative and go directly after Popeyes for bragging rights on who makes better "spicy" chicken. Internal comparative research justified Church's claim and marketing direction.

With its agency, Cartel Creativo, Church's decided to approach the initiative with humor while maintaining Church's definitive claim of "spicy" ownership. The challenge that lay ahead for Church's was not only taking a more aggressive stance but to communicate its positioning to its multicultural consumer base, which consisted of one-third African Americans, one-third Latinos, and one-third Anglos.

The key was to deliver the single message of "spicy" ownership in a manner that would be relevant to each consumer's cultural background and mindset. In general, humor is a delicate balance to maintain, but when communicating to multiple cultures, there is that danger of losing something in the translation. To quote Clifton Fadiman, "a sense of humor is the ability to understand a joke—and that the joke is oneself."

The Latino segment would add to the challenge in that Church's takes into consideration the market as whole: both the acculturated and the un-acculturated.

So developing a culturally relevant message that is fun, humorous and engaging to all three segments, while being cognizant of the duality of the Latino market is easier said than done.

Insights

With Cartel Creativo's CultureView™ approach, Church's was able to gain access to the Latino market through key insights that help bridge consumer and corporate cultural gaps.

- Translations often connote little interest from the brand to the Latino consumer. It demonstrates that a brand does not want to take the time to understand the cultural nuances to optimally communicate their brand message. Western abstract humor may not communicate so well to unacculturated Latinos; humor needs to be culturally relevant.

If Coke is the "real" thing, what exactly is "real" to a Latino? KFC is authentic Southern fried chicken, but what does "Southern" mean to a Latino? Nike says to "Just do it." What exactly are unacculturated Latinos suppose to do?

• The acculturation model is outdated; assimilation is no longer the end goal. Latinos are not taking that last step and very much want to keep their culture viable. So it's important to demonstrate a sense of cultural acknowledgment if not cultural celebration. Relying on the casting and some cultural cues is neither commitment nor a solution.

• It may not be "retro", but some acculturated Latinos are rediscovering their cultures and making their "Latinoness" a point of pride. Where once English was good enough to get a general market message across, now brands must demonstrate cultural knowledge. Acculturated Latinos are aware of their equity, and brands must demonstrate that cultural insight to break through the clutter.

• Ricky Martin may have been a fad but "Latino" is here to stay. The Latino culture is growing and solidifying through cultural rediscovery, natural growth, generational traditions, and being replenished by immigration. So are you confident enough that your general market message is connecting with acculturated Latinos? Church's did not want to wait for un-acculturated Latinos to catch up to acculturated Latinos?

• Unacculturated Latinos do not have a history of who Church's is as a brand here in the USA; they need to learn who you are. Even if you have a presence in their country of origin, what they experience there is not what they will experience here. Church's is always aware that their communication to uncultivated Latino includes education and awareness.

Campaign Objectives

To communicate to Church's multicultural segments, including Latinos at all levels of acculturation, that they have the best tasting spicy chicken and internal taste tests show that Popeyes and Church's customers like Church's spicy chicken better than Popeyes'.

• To reinforce Church's in the top of mind of the consumer that they have the best Spicy Chicken

• To encourage trial of Church's spicy chicken among shared guests and new customers

• To create awareness for the spicy chicken at Church's among competitive users of QSR chicken category and grow market share

CASESTUDY   CHURCH'S CHICKEN (CONT.)

- To generate enough buzz and trial to get the brand over the one-year rollover date. Church's was competing against double-digit increases in both sales and transactions.

Target Audience

The primary target for the "truly spicy" campaign was 25 to 34, low-income African American, Latino, and Anglo segments. A secondary target was 18 to 24 that skewed more male. The target consumers were "spicy" experts, consumers who really knew their spicy chicken products and would act as influencers. The profile also included variety seekers with an adventurous attitude.

For unacculturated Latinos the key was to seek those who were familiar with fried chicken and "spicy" but not necessarily knowledgeable about "American" fried chicken. History was not more important than connecting with their taste motivators. Church's knew how important "spicy" or "picante" is to the Latino cuisine.

Creative Strategy

The creative strategy was direct in that it would demonstrate, through humor, consumers being put through a lie detector test by clinical experts to determine which spicy flavor consumers prefer—Church's or Popeyes. The tests were set on the public streets for a "man on the street" feel.

The direction derived from the insight that African Americans are skeptical of messages coming from corporations directly. For Latinos, the insight was how important word of mouth and trusted advisors are to them when considering brands, particularly un-acculturated Latinos. The campaign was built directly from the consumer's viewpoint. Consumers would see themselves in the spots.

When developing the spots, strict attention was given to casting, dialogue and social interaction. It was paramount that the consumers saw themselves in the spots and not models that would take them out of their world—this was the voice of the consumer.

The interaction played off African-American and Latino couples and Popeyes' employees who wanted to please their partners or employers by choosing their respective chicken and being exposed to really preferring Church's.

For Latinos, the interaction of the couples was careful to create situations that would be familiar to them in their lives and that they could relate to as Latinos. To follow through on commitment and cultural knowledge of the various acculturation levels of Latinos, the spots where created in English, Spanish, and a mix of Spanglish. Though there are

CHURCH'S CHICKEN (CONT.)

naysayers in the Latino advertising and marketing communities about using "Spanglish," it is, nonetheless, a reality in the Latino market. Church's goal is always to demonstrate an understanding of its consumer's environment. An example of the commitment was also evident in how the Latinos are portrayed in the spots. Latinos were always aspirational, not unattainable, but in a positive light. The dialogue was realistic, but not so provincial as to alienate the full spectrum of the market.

The goal was to deliver moments that would communicate fun, knowledge, Latino flavor, and the brand's relevancy in the Latino market.

Media Strategies

In Church's key Latino markets (Texas, New Mexico, and Arizona) the message was communicated in both English and Spanish using television and radio. Following the strategy, the communications in Spanish were not "translations" of the English message but presented in a relevant manner that is both socially and culturally accessible.

For radio, the plan was to cover the full listening spectrum of the Latino market and Church's core Latino consumer (18 to 45). The formats chosen were indicative of both the markets (cities) and the listening palates of the Latino consumer.

Church's direction is not to acknowledge the Latino community but celebrate the culture as part of our American landscape, to demonstrate knowledge and understanding of its Latino consumer.

Evidence of Results / Summary

In a heated competitive environment the "Lie Detector" campaign elicited immediate attention from the QSR category and was hailed as a well-executed, gusty endeavor with a strong selling proposition. The campaign also garnered itself advertising awards (ADDY). *Nation's Restaurant News* named the campaign the #1 competitive/comparative spot for 2006.

Church's Sales numbers for the third quarter were strong and showed immediate results. Sales were positive even though the brand was being compared with over double digits increases in sales and transactions from the year before.

The campaign brought forth Church's as a more serious candidate in the spicy chicken battle. With Latinos, Church's continued to establish a relationship where they could demonstrate a key desire to grow with the segment. Church's was able to build a strong awareness and differentiate itself with the Latino segment.

CHAPTER 9

The Youth Segments

Los Bebés: Age 0 to 5
Sub-Segment Size: 5.3 million (12 percent)

The youngest of the Latino age segments—over 5.3 million Latino babies and toddlers aged 0 to 5 years—will live in a different world than their older siblings. Most of them will be raised in acculturated households with computers and at least one family member will be able to navigate the web in Spanish as well as in English.

The vast majority of Los Bebés are native-born—95 percent were born in the U.S. and 52 percent were born to foreign-born parents who migrated to the U.S. Given the growing recognition and value of multiculturalism in a global economy and the growing maturity of Spanish-language education and media, it is highly possible that most of these Bebés will grow to be fluent in English, and in many cases bilingual.

FIGURE 9.1 . . . .

GenAge Segments: Los Bebès, Aged 0 to 5, 2006

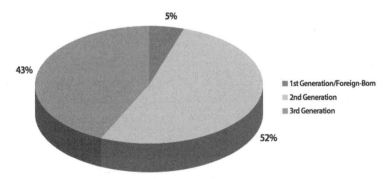

- 1st Generation/Foreign-Born
- 2nd Generation
- 3rd Generation

Source: M. Isabel Valdés. The 2006 data is consistent with independent estimates including those from the Pew Hispanic Center and the Census Bureau's 2006 March Current Population Survey, Annual Social and Economic Supplement, ©2007.

FIGURE 9.2 . . . .

GenAge Segments: Los Bebès Aged 0 to 5, 2006

(in thousands)

TOTAL BEBÉS	1ST GENERATION/ FOREIGN-BORN	U.S.-BORN TOTAL	2ND GENERATION	3RD GENERATION OR GREATER
5,346	262	5,084	2,765	2,319
100%	5%	95%	52%	43%

Source: M. Isabel Valdés. The 2006 data is consistent with independent estimates including those from the Pew Hispanic Center and the Census Bureau's 2006 March Current Population Survey, Annual Social and Economic Supplement, ©2007.

Marketing to Los Bebés—and Their Moms

Judging from the growing marketing activity targeting new Hispanic moms, and the proliferation of preschool television cartoons in Spanish, corporate America has discovered at last the value of the youngest Latino citizens. Not only are traditional advertisers developing programs to appeal to these moms, more players are entering the market, including consumer products, toys, health care and pharmaceuticals, the financial sectors, magazines, and the online world.

FIGURE 9.3 . . . .

Hispanic Fertility Rates, 2005

	WOMEN WITH A BIRTH IN THE PAST YEAR	% OF WOMEN WITH A BIRTH IN THE PAST YEAR	SHARE OF WOMEN WITH A BIRTH IN THE PAST YEAR
Total Hispanic	900,729	9.2%	21.3%
U.S.-born Hispanic	397,133	7.9%	9.4%
Foreign-born/First-generation Hispanic	503,596	10.5%	11.9%
Total U.S.	4,222,080	7.0%	100.0%

Source: Hispanics at Mid-Decade, Pew Hispanic Center tabulations of 2005 American Community Survey.

Talking to the expectant or new mom is a perfect "POE," or point-of-entry venue, coveted by savvy marketers. Finding the new Latina mom is now easier than ever before. Hospitals in high-density, new-immigrant Hispanic areas are glad to distribute samples and educational materials in Spanish or English to new Hispanic moms, since it helps them inform and communicate with these patients. There are also several pre-natal magazines, dedicated online websites, sections in TV, radio programs and newspaper articles. These dedicated media talk to the specific needs and wants of the Latina mom, and they do it in-culture! For example, *Espera* is a pre-natal Spanish-language magazine designed to communicate with the non-acculturated Latina mom-to-be. Included among many others as advertisers in the first issue of *Espera*, with over 350,000 copies sent to obstetricians and gynecologists, are Johnson & Johnson, Huggies, Nestlé, and Playtex. Another such publication, *Lamaze Para Padres*, has more than tripled its original circulation to over 750,000. A popular magazine read by Latina moms at the clinic or hospitals, *Primeros Doce Meses*, is an annual by American Baby Group with half a million in circulation. As mentioned above, clinics, hospitals and primary-school PTA's are excellent places to distribute samples for new or repeat Latina moms.

Online, several dedicated sites talk to the new Hispanic mom, such as www.todobebe.com. As Internet use grows among Latina moms, marketers and advertisers are including websites in their marketing mix. For another example, see www.nacersano.org, a Spanish-language website developed by JMCP's March of Dimes/Folic Acid education campaign.

Los Niños: Aged 6 to 9
Sub-Segment Size: 3.3 million (7 percent)

Between 2001 and 2010, the percentage of Hispanic children aged 5 to 9 will increase by 21 percent, while the share of non-Hispanic white and black children will continue to decline steadily. This demographic shift will continue to fuel the growing diversity in America's grade schools. The pressure to deliver high quality education added to the increasing numbers of students from different cultural backgrounds in already crowded classrooms will push schools to find solutions. *American Demographics* (September, 2000) predicts many schools will "mass customize" education, delivering educational materials to meet the specific needs and interests of each student using new computer-based technologies.

Fortunately, many Latino children are becoming computer literate and at a fast pace. As access to a computer at school or at home continues to grow, Los Niños press their parents to get a home computer and then often the children teach their parents how to go online.

FIGURE 9.4 . . . .

GenAge Segments: Los Niños, Aged 6 to 9, 2006

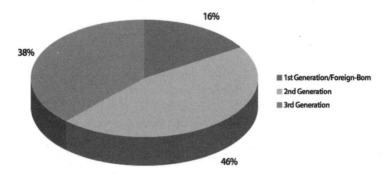

Source: M. Isabel Valdés. The 2006 data is consistent with independent estimates including those from the Pew Hispanic Center and the Census Bureau's 2006 March Current Population Survey, Annual Social and Economic Supplement, ©2007.

FIGURE 9.5 . . . .

GenAge Segments: Los Niños Aged 6 to 9, 2006

(in thousands)

TOTAL NIÑOS	1ST GENERATION/ FOREIGN-BORN	U.S.-BORN TOTAL	2ND GENERATION	3RD GENERATION OR GREATER
3,254	422	2,832	1,495	1,337
100%	13%	87%	46%	41%

Source: M. Isabel Valdés. The 2006 data is consistent with independent estimates including those from the Pew Hispanic Center and the Census Bureau's 2006 March Current Population Survey, Annual Social and Economic Supplement, ©2007.

Marketing to Los Niños—and Their Moms

Los Niños exert great influence on their parents' brand and product preferences, leisure-time plans and vacations, as well as on their families' entertainment choices of DVDs, videos, amusement parks, and films. However, their influence can be even stronger than that of their non-Hispanic counterparts, since the vast majority of Los Niños (65 percent) are born to foreign-born parents. These Latino parents are improving their socioeconomic status steadily, and, as previously mentioned, are sensitive to the "nag factor" and their "compensatory" feelings. In addition, many tend to hold traditional Hispanic cultural values where "the child is king," also referred to as Chicoismo.[1]

Los Niños as Marketers

In the case of foreign-born parents, Los Niños tend to play a key role in introducing their families to new products and brands. As they visit their non-Hispanic friends' households, they learn about new foods, computer games, technology, and other products and services not yet promoted via Spanish-language media. In cases where parents have limited English, Los Niños help translate for their elders in many social situations, from interactions with authorities and doctors, to directions for preparing a recipe. Marketers many times "talk" to Niños in their media messages in order to get the Latina mom or dad to act, in what I call the two-step communications approach.

Los Niños and Language

Given that 87 percent of Los Niños are born in the U.S. and go to grade school in the U.S., their non-Latino peers at school will have an impact not only on their language use and preference, but also their cultural value orientation. In highly concentrated Hispanic urban areas, such as East Los Angeles, Coral Gables in Miami, Corona in Queens, and Washington Heights in New York, children interact closely with other Latino children. More than with previous generations of Latinos, child peers help them be more comfortable with their Latino culture and in speaking Spanish outside the home. School systems around the country, with few exceptions, have a much more supportive attitude towards children of diverse backgrounds, and many actually have programs to make these young immigrants feel special and at home. As a consequence, the Niño generation will grow to be bilingual and bicultural, and in most cases, maintain traditional Hispanic value orientation. This observation is less the case with Latino children residing in lower-density Hispanic population areas—usually suburbs with higher incomes. These children are exposed mostly to an Anglo value-oriented culture and speak mostly English with their friends and peers. Depending on the parents' pressure, they may or may not speak Spanish at home.

Another venue is corporate contributions for scholarship funds—and promoting these to the Hispanic community.

Retailers and manufacturers aware of the pull Latino children have on parents' purchase behavior are increasingly partnering to attract this young lucrative segment with programs that give something to all. For example, Kraft used an innovative approach to introduce its new pizza and build *Share of Heart*. Managers of Tombstone Pizza, Kraft's new Mexican Style pizza, partnered with Spanish-language radio KHCK-FM in Dallas, the Six Flags Theme Park, and Albertson's grocery stores. Luis Sosa, a "10-year-old veteran" at the radio station invited young listeners to participate and win. For each purchase of two Tombstone Mexican Style pizzas, KHCK listeners received a free all-day pass to Six Flags. The instant redemption offers were redeemed during KHCK-FM's van visits at 12 different Albertson's locations from 4 to 5 p.m. each weekday. The promotion's success was overwhelming. "To make it effective, we needed to sell 4,000 pizzas. We ended up selling over 10,000!" said Mark Vosberg, Dallas Kraft Planning Manager.[3] The product and promotion's media and family fun mix had great appeal to kids as well as the elements to talk to their parents' hearts and wallets.

A successful campaign by Anheuser-Busch demonstrates how manufacturers of sensitive products, in this case beer, can win Share of Heart with Hispanic families. Certainly the beer manufacturer does not want to promote its alcoholic beverages to minors, nor does the company want to miss out on the opportunity to build Share of Heart with targeted Hispanic families. So Anheuser-Busch teamed up with Major League Baseball teams, including the Los Angeles Dodgers, Florida Marlins, Houston Astros, and New York Yankees, all key Hispanic markets. They created the Homerunazo Scholarship Campaign. Budweiser donated $100 to the Hispanic scholarship fund for every home run hit by participating teams during the 2001 season. By being a good neighbor and giving back to the community, the brand, Budweiser, built Share of Heart without even selling its product.

Generation Ñ: Aged 10 to 19
Segment Size: 7.6 million (17 percent)

Generation Ñ is probably the most written about and coveted Hispanic market segment today. At more than 6 million in size, this group is living fully "the best of both worlds." Media, entertainment channels, music producers, manufacturers of apparel foods, beverages, and even cars are targeting Latino Tweens and Teens, and through them, their parents.

Generation Ñ includes the group aged 10 to 19: transitioning tweens, teens, and young adults. More than their predecessors, they are generally bilingual and open to adapting to the American way of life. At the same time, they are proud of their Latino heritage and do not want to lose their Hispanic identity.

A study by Teenage Research Unlimited in June 2001 said, "Latino youths shop more and outspend their counterparts in the non-Latino world—despite coming from lower-income families. The average Hispanic teen spends $320 a month, 4 percent more than the average non-Hispanic teen. Favorite shopping outlets are malls (84 percent), supermarkets (80 percent) and discount chains (78 percent)."[2]

FIGURE 9.6 . . . .

GenAge Segments: Generation Ñ, Aged 10 to 19, 2006

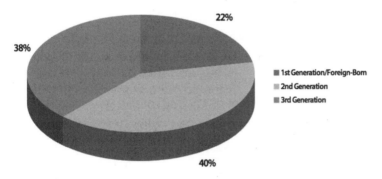

Source: M. Isabel Valdés. The 2006 data is consistent with independent estimates including those from the Pew Hispanic Center and the Census Bureau's 2006 March Current Population Survey, Annual Social and Economic Supplement, ©2007.

With an estimated $19 billion in spending power, Gen Ñ is not only changing the content of Hispanic TV, radio, and print media, but also general market media. That is because one-half of the U.S. Latino population is under age 26, compared with age 39 for non-Hispanic whites.

This segment is presently leading the growth in the under age 18 category in the United States. While the non-Hispanic youth growth rate continues to decline, the Latino segment has grown exponentially. One in five teens in the United States is of Hispanic descent. Between 2005 and 2020 the Latino teen population is expected to grow 35.6 percent, compared with a decline of 2.6 percent among non-Hispanic whites.

FIGURE 9.7 . . . .

GenAge Segments: Generation Ñ, Aged 10 to 19, 2006

(in thousands)

TOTAL GENERATION Ñ	1ST GENERATION/ FOREIGN-BORN	U.S. BORN TOTAL	2ND GENERATION	3RD GENERATION OR GREATER
7,577	1,644	5,933	3,078	2,855
100%	22%	88%	40%	38%

Source: M. Isabel Valdés. The 2006 data is consistent with independent estimates including those from the Pew Hispanic Center and the Census Bureau's 2006 March Current Population Survey, Annual Social and Economic Supplement, ©2007.

Marketing to Gen Ñ

From a marketing perspective, Generation Ñ has the importance of American Baby Boomers when they were in their "Woodstock" years. These young consumers are adopting brands and making them their own. Marketers who fail to attract this generation today may have lost them for their adult spending years. Many corporations that are aware of Gen Ñ's economic clout through influencing their parents and the long-term benefit to their brands, target Gen Ñ, in Spanish, English, and/or in both languages, since teens tend to move quickly back and forth between languages.

However, the psychological differences within this age segment are too broad for easy definition. Their interests, likes, dislikes, and aspirations require a subdivision of the group. Therefore, Gen Ñ is subdivided into two groups, usually Tweens and Teens.

For example, statistics show that one in five Latinas in this age group attempts suicide. Luis H. Zayas, Ph.D., professor of social work at Washington University in St. Louis, has developed a research model to better understand this phenomenon. The issues described in Marianismo, in which Latinas are expected to defer to their parents, may put these adolescents in conflict with the cultural values of mainstream America to such an extent that it leads to depression and suicide.

According to the Association of Hispanic Advertising Agencies (AHAA), the estimated 6.3 million Latinos aged 10-19 represent 20 percent of the entire U.S. youth population and spend about $20 billion a year. Latino youth also represent a huge market for the media and technology sectors. Recent data released by Simmons Research for Yahoo! Telemundo showed that Hispanic youth spend over 32 hours of their waking week engaged in media and technology, whether that be surfing the internet, watching TV, talking on their cell phones, or as is frequently the case, doing all at the same time, which accounts for the seemingly impossible amount of time recorded for such activities.

In line with their tech-savvy, Hispanic youth are also very connected online. Social networking sites are hugely popular places for them to chat, share music, flirt, etc. Urban themes are prevalent in the culture as is reflected by the musical styles that are most popular among them, namely Reggaeton and Hip-Hop. This urban focus is in turn reflected by the advertising campaigns targeting this group.

However, Latino youth are not a monolithic and separate group from their non-Hispanic peers—not by a long shot. They are interwoven into the very fabric of the larger youth culture in the U.S. and are represented in every subgroup imaginable on some level. They identify with the culture of their parents from their at-home experience where Spanish is primarily spoken, while their time online and at school lends itself to mainstream tendencies and English-language interaction. As such, the Latino youth experience is bicultural at the core.

ATENCIÓN

4 Things Indispensable to Today's Hispanic Teen

- Cell Phone
- Music: Reggaeton/Hip-Hop reign supreme
- Hip clothing
- Friends: social networks

Trends In Hispanic Youth Marketing

- Relevant music: Hip-Hop/Reggaeton
- Urban Themes: street life, surroundings
- Interactivity: one-way messaging no longer sufficient for the young audience.
- Online: where it's at

Tweens: Aged 10 to 14
Sub-Segment Size: 4.0 million (9 percent)

Latino tweens, aged 10 to 14, are at the center of the swelling growth of Hispanic youth, significantly outpacing the growth rate of all other Hispanic and non-Hispanic age groups (except Asian youth).

FIGURE 9.8 . . . .

GenAge Segments: Tweens, Aged 10 to 14, 2006

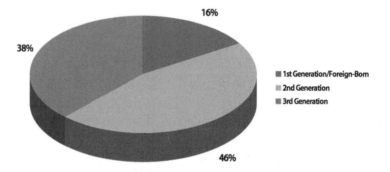

Source: M. Isabel Valdés. The 2006 data is consistent with independent estimates including those from the Pew Hispanic Center and the Census Bureau's 2006 March Current Population Survey, Annual Social and Economic Supplement, ©2007.

FIGURE 9.9 . . . .

GenAge Segments: Tweens, Aged 10 to 14, 2006

(in thousands)

TOTAL TWEENS	1ST GENERATION/ FOREIGN-BORN	U.S.-BORN TOTAL	2ND GENERATION	3RD GENERATION OR GREATER
3,977	646	3,331	1,804	1,527
100%	16%	84%	46%	38%

Source: M. Isabel Valdés. The 2006 data is consistent with independent estimates including those from the Pew Hispanic Center and the Census Bureau's 2006 March Current Population Survey, Annual Social and Economic Supplement, ©2007.

Like the younger Latinos (Los Bebés and Los Niños), 84 percent were born in the U.S; however, most (62 percent) were born to foreign-born parents. They represent 16 percent of the total U.S. Hispanic population.

Although this generation of Hispanic tweens is growing closer experientially and psychographically to general market teens, it will take more than one generation to stave off the strong Familismo bonds and family interactions. For example, Latino tweens tend to be more dependent on their parents than their

Anglo counterparts. This phenomenon helps explain, in part, the strong adherence to traditional Hispanic value orientation observed in older acculturated Latinos and Latinas.

Chicoismo, as mentioned earlier, is a powerful Hispanic cultural value that centers the child at the core of the family's dynamic. In fact, many Hispanic immigrant parents say the main reason behind their immigration to the U.S. is to provide their children with opportunities for a better life. The parents therefore tend to expect more attention, social time, and support from their children. In other words, these family-centered cultural values are a two-way street that opens marketing opportunities to both children and parents.

Hispanic Teens: Aged 15 to 19
Sub-Segment Size: 3.6 million (8 percent)

The older group of Generation Ñ, Latino teens aged 15 to 19, will continue the dramatic growth experienced during the past decade. Mostly bilingual and bicultural, they may look like other teens to the outside world, and in many ways, they are like general market teens. However, culturally speaking, these teens are highly bicultural as mentioned above, and they move swiftly between two cultures. Most are proud to be Latinos, ready to "show-off" their Hispanic roots. Many have embraced a best-of-both-world's attitude. Today's teens are leading the dramatic growth of U.S.-born Latino consumers. Of all Hispanic teens, 72 percent are native-born. Just over one-half are born to recent immigrant parents (55 percent) while a large segment have U.S.-born, third and fourth generation parents (20 percent and 25 percent, respectively).

There is a tremendous variation in terms of value orientation, language preference and socioeconomic status within the Generation Ñ segment—between teens born to long-term, deep-rooted Hispanic parents of several generations and teens born to recently immigrated parents. Most teens born to deep-rooted parents have the advantage of parents who know English well, have a complete picture of U.S. society, and can guide them in their homework, help them in college preparation, and so forth. In contrast, teens born to first generation immigrant parents who are themselves adjusting and learning the ropes, in many cases with little or no command of English, face unique challenges and disadvantages. This results in additional frustrations and stress to the typical teenagers' life and higher school dropout rates.

Two national foundations, the Lilly Endowment, Inc. and the Bill and

Melinda Gates Foundation contributed $50 million each to the Hispanic Scholarship Fund (HSF). In addition, corporations like Philip Morris, PepsiCo, Frito-Lay, Anheuser-Busch, Coca-Cola, AOL Time Warner, Univision, Disney and many others contribute with scholarship funds and support educational programs for Latinos. The marketing return on investment is enormous. I have observed from many market research studies that brand recall tends to be significantly higher when promotions contain an educational component.

FIGURE 9.10 ....

GenAge Segments: Teens Aged 15–19, 2006

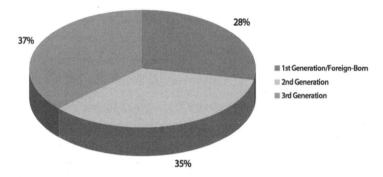

Source: M. Isabel Valdés. The 2006 data is consistent with independent estimates including those from the Pew Hispanic Center and the Census Bureau's 2006 March Current Population Survey, Annual Social and Economic Supplement, ©2007.

FIGURE 9.11 ....

GenAge Segments: Teens Aged 15 to 19, 2006

(in thousands)

TOTAL TEENS	1ST GENERATION/ FOREIGN-BORN	U.S.-BORN TOTAL	2ND GENERATION	3RD GENERATION OR GREATER
3,599	998	2,601	1,273	1,328
100%	28%	72%	35%	37%

Source: M. Isabel Valdés. The 2006 data is consistent with independent estimates including those from the Pew Hispanic Center and the Census Bureau's 2006 March Current Population Survey, Annual Social and Economic Supplement, ©2007.

CASESTUDY   MONTEREY BAY AQUARIUM, 2006 HISPANIC GUESTS

Background

Monterey Bay Aquarium's attendance by the general market has leveled off at about 1.7 million visitors per year. Although the aquarium attracts an international audience, 64 percent of the visitors come from California. Managers of the aquarium decided to focus on Hispanics in 2006 because they believe the facility should reflect the California population which will be 40 percent Hispanic by 2015. They also wanted to tap into this market segment's rapid fiscal growth, and to inspire more Hispanic kids and their families to protect our oceans. The number of Hispanics visiting the aquarium reached its height in 2004 when there were more than 97,000 Hispanic visitors but the increased attendance was due to the first white shark at the facility. By 2006, Hispanic visitors had returned to previous attendance levels.

Of the Hispanic visitors, about one third are from the San Francisco Bay area., 11 percent are from Fresno, 26 percent from Southern California, and 13 percent from elsewhere in Northern California. Only about 5 percent of Hispanics are from the local market. Seventy percent of all Hispanic adults visit with children, whereas only 40 percent of non-Hispanic adults visit with children. As a group, Hispanic visitors tend to be younger than non-Hispanic visitors. Thirty-seven percent of Hispanic visitors speak Spanish all or most of the time while at home; one-third speak Spanish just some of the time; and 22 percent do not speak Spanish.

Objectives

To attract more Hispanic visitors

In-Culture Strategies

The aquarium's strategy was to craft events that were of cultural relevance, including commissioning a popular theater group El Teatro Campesino to present a skit about plastics. *Basta Basura* (*Enough Trash*) premiered during Fiesta del Mar.

Special events in 2006 included:

Día del Niño (April 23)—Day of the Child

Hispanic Heritage Day (September 9)— Kicked off Hispanic Heritage month, where a "Hero of the Environment" award was given to Mexican soccer star, Jorge Campos.

Fiesta del Mar (October 16)—Celebration of the Ocean, where a "Hero of the Environment" award was given to Mexican pop star, Emmanuel.

Marketing results

2006 marks the first time that Hispanic attendance exceeded 50 percent of total visitors during two of the special events: Day of the Child and Fiesta Del Mar. The three Hispanic special events days combined attracted more than 12,000 Hispanic visitors. The special events attracted a different Hispanic segment (more Spanish-speakers, lower household income) and more Hispanic visitors picked up information about protecting the oceans during the special events.

Marketing to Hispanic Teens

HispanTelligence, the research division of Hispanic Business, Inc., estimates that Hispanics aged 16 to 24 have purchasing power of more than $25 million. "An investor dreams of finding a trend like this," said a San Francisco-based merchant banker.

Marketers have learned that general market translation or adaptation does not work when targeting Hispanics, and teens are particularly sensitive to this issue. "Latino teens are really bicultural," said Giuseppi D'Alesandro, former senior marketing manager of PepsiCo. Latino youth are increasingly targeted by English-language media; however, many seem to relate to traditional Hispanic programming and enjoy it more than English-language programming.

Understanding Hispanic culture and reflecting their values and beliefs in ads for Hispanic teens can make or break the ad. This Latino teen culture is a hybrid of the general market teen and the Latino "barrio teen" culture that can also vary by U.S. region. It's not just about being bicultural. As with their younger siblings, Latinos entered primary school later in life and many reside at their parents' home longer than their Anglo counterparts do, as is traditional in Hispanic culture. They feel the pull of Familismo, the strong Hispanic family orientation, sometimes at odds with the lifestyles and values of their non-Hispanic peers. Often this dichotomy leads them to a conflict of allegiances. Because second, third, and fourth or greater generations of Hispanics tend to concentrate in the Southwest, more "acculturated" teens tend to concentrate in these markets, for example, San Antonio, Dallas, Phoenix, and El Paso.

To deal with these complex advertising challenges, AHAA (*www.ahaa.org*) publishes a directory of the names of specialized advertising and PR agencies, market researchers, promotion agencies, consultants and media reps. This organization can be extremely helpful to marketers and business decision-makers in putting together a successful Latino teen advertising and marketing program.

When researching Latino teens, it becomes apparent that they are facing even more stress than non-immigrant youth. The Washington, D.C.–based Urban Institute conducted longitudinal analysis looking at ten common risk behaviors that affect teens' health and well-being. Hispanic teens in grades 9 through 12 showed less of a decline in these risk behaviors than their black and white non-Hispanic counterparts. The share of Hispanic teens that engaged in five or more risk behaviors was nearly double.

As in the case of corporate presence in education, there are other areas where community marketing can focus. For example, helping build sports arenas in the inner city or creating awards for teens that excel in soccer or other sports. Again, by sponsoring youth-related activities, corporations create win-win-win marketing links with the Latino teens and their families. One such highly successful case is that of Honda of America. Following the advice of its Hispanic ad agency of record, la Agencia de Orci y Asociados, Honda was the first company to sponsor the soccer World Cup in the United States and create the U.S. Soccer Player Award as an integral component of its marketing and advertising program. The results, measured in the increase in actual car sales, was enormous (see Chapter 6).

Campaign: Velocidad al Ritmo de Tu Vida
Agency: Fleishman-Hillard

The Challenge

When AT&T (then SBC Communications, Inc.) wanted to increase its share of high-speed Internet DSL service in suburban and smaller communities in 2005, it encountered an unexpected barrier. The company's then 13-state footprint included such key states as California, Texas, and Illinois with high growth customer acquisition opportunities in small cities and suburban neighborhoods, but many of these areas had a mostly Hispanic population, ranging from 45 percent to 90 percent. These cities also had a high concentration of Spanish-preferred consumers, many of whom were not familiar with DSL or perceived it as an expensive service. In addition, roughly 35 percent of these consumers were accustomed to a dial-up connection. Also, internal research and market savvy provided insight that traditional advertising alone was not going to persuade Spanish-dominant or bilingual Hispanic consumers to invest in DSL.

Finally, when compared with advertising, public relations was a more effective and cost effective way reach these markets.

In 2005, key findings from U.S. Hispanic market reports showed that:

- More than half (53 percent) of offline Hispanics expected to get an Internet connection at home within the next two years.

- Eight in 10 online Hispanics used the Internet regularly to communicate with friends and family.

- More than three in four online Hispanics with children who went online (79 percent) said that the Internet had a positive effect on the skills their children will need for a successful career.

- Hispanics used the Internet to a greater degree than the general online population in listening to music and instant messaging

To help overcome barriers in expanding DSL to rural general market communities, Fleishman-Hillard (FH) and SBC created a successful general market grassroots/public relations campaign dubbed Hometown Tour. The program was built on the approach of visiting local communities to conduct intensive demonstrations, town hall meetings, and audience-engaging initiatives that helped would-be DSL customers experience the technology's applications first hand. Adapting the program to Spanish-speaking communities seemed like the best approach to helping Hispanic consumers gain knowledge of the service.

HOMETOWN TOUR PARA TI: AT&T (CONT.)

Two key elements needed for the Hispanic market program were:

1. emphasis on one-on-one personal contact with the consumer in Spanish that would also help position AT&T as a community resource; and,

2. focus on education regarding new culturally relevant technologies and communication tools that were enhanced and enabled by higher Internet connection speeds.

The Solution

Working with internal research to address the challenge of capturing Spanish-dominant Hispanic consumers in key growth markets, FH and AT&T created the Hometown Tour Para Ti program—a Hispanic-focused grassroots initiative with very strong media appeal.

In selecting cities to be included in the tour, FH and AT&T focused on town and suburban neighborhoods with at least a 30 percent Hispanic population, the market's DSL growth potential, availability of DSL service, and the availability of local Univision/Telemundo TV affiliates, radio stations with Hispanic-focused community programming, and Spanish-language or bilingual publications.

A total of 12 communities were selected, including all major U.S. towns along the Texas-Mexico border; La Villita/Pilsen Hispanic neighborhood in Chicago; Waukegan, Ill; two southern California communities including San Diego; two northern California communities; and Reno, Nevada.

The program's concept revolved around the notion of "speed at the pace of your life" or "Velocidad al Ritmo de tu Vida" and was structured to primarily target three important audiences:

- Hispanic homeowners and small business owners, aged 25 to 45, with school-age children and Hispanic consumers currently using dial-up Internet service.
- Hispanic community leaders and educators in elementary school districts with a high percentage of Hispanic student enrollment.
- Local Hispanic and mainstream media.

The tour was then planned as a layered approach to demonstrate the benefits of DSL to different subgroups among the Hispanic population, depending on their interests. Program elements included:

- Interactive Technology Demonstrations: Bilingual presentations of the features of DSL that offered a chance to interact with the latest electronics made popular because of a high-speed Internet connection, including digital music players and cameras, security

CASESTUDY — HOMETOWN TOUR PARA TI: AT&T (CONT.)

cameras, Web cams, and even a robotic dog. The tour partnered with Hispanic chambers of commerce and other community organizations to reach out to their members and help drive attendance.

- School Outreach: Visits to elementary schools providing free, teacher-approved, interactive lessons designed to teach kids about online safety. These visits reached 500 to 800 students per tour stop. Teachers were provided with a tool kit of CD-ROMs, award certificates for the students who completed the lesson, and safety tip sheets for schools to incorporate the lesson into their curriculums, if desired.

- Media Partner/Media Briefings/Desk Side Visits: Events were promoted through value-add media partnerships with local Univision TV and radio affiliates. To promote media coverage, FH issued localized advisories, developed media kits, and set up meetings with key reporters personally inviting them to the events.

- Para Ti Spanish-language Web site and DSL Demo: On AT&T's Spanish-language consumer website, FH developed a Spanish-language campaign "sitelet" featuring the key benefits and pricing for DSL, an interactive flash demonstration of the features of the service (also produced as a CD-ROM to distribute at events), tour schedule, and pages featuring photos and journal entries of the completed visits.

The tour's execution was led by bilingual "tour guides," Hispanic marketing specialists on the AT&T corporate communications team who enabled the demonstrations, led the presentations, coordinated all local activities, and engaged local influencers and AT&T local teams in tour stops. Each presentation also was enhanced with Spanish-language collateral and promotional premiums, including brochures, fact sheets, posters, direct mail postcards sent to consumers' homes to promote tour visits, and branded giveaways.

The Results

The Hometown Tour Para Ti effectively engaged target Hispanic communities with consumer-centric strategies and activities that helped increase new DSL line activations an average of 30 percent across all Hispanic communities following the tour visits.

Tour visits also generated more than 5 million media impressions, including a complete feature on Univision's Chicago technology segment "*El Pulso Tecnológico*," live interviews on TV and radio, and positive stories about the tour's visits in Hispanic weeklies and mainstream community papers, including a front page story in *The Eagle Pass Business Journal*.

HOMETOWN TOUR PARA TI: AT&T (CONT.)

Across all tour stops, the tour reached a total audience of more than 6,500 consumers and students with in-person, bilingual technology demonstrations and Internet safety classes.

Additionally, the tour provided a forum for strengthening AT&T's reputation among Hispanic community leaders and generated support for Hometown Tour Para Ti visits in their towns. For example, the Mayor of McAllen, Texas,, introduced the tour and attended the technology demonstration in association with the local Hispanic chamber of commerce. Also in McAllen, the Independent School District, was so impressed with the Internet safety program that they requested the event in all of the district's 18 elementary schools. The same request was made from the instructional technology coordinator for the Eagle Pass, Texas, Independent School District who asked for the presentation in the district's 14 elementary schools.

CHAPTER 10

The Adult Segments

Latinas and Latinos: Aged 20 to 39
Segment Size: 15.5 million (35 percent)

Young Hispanic adults, aged 20 to 39, are in their main household formation years. About 17.3 percent of U.S. Hispanics are in their twenties, and another 17.3 percent are in their thirties. They are responsible in part for the growing Latino baby boom, as they begin to have families and settle down. By the time they reach age 39, about one-half will be married and 12.6 percent divorced. Thirty-seven percent are either single or not "legally" married. ("Common law" marriage is more common among low income Hispanics, and in the rural areas in Latin America.) Someone in this age group heads 4.5 percent of Hispanic households.

- Over half (60 percent) are foreign-born

- And 40 percent were born in the U.S. with their parents or grandparents also born in the United States.

Of the consumers in their family formation years, this is the youngest and first GenAge segment likely to be more bilingual and more acculturated. Based on the estimates of year of arrival, it is highly probable that those who are foreign-born completed at least some of their schooling in the U.S. and have been in contact every day with the mainstream culture. Should we treat them as "acculturated" Hispanics, with no roots, no "two-culture pride?" Probably not. From their initial social interaction, these young Latinos and Latinas might make you believe they are 100 percent assimilated. However, at the core, in their inner soul and mind, they probably deal with many stressors reflective of the effort the—and their parents—have to expend in order to live a "normal" life in the U.S., their new host country.

Health statistics show that young Latinos and Latinas have more instances of depression and alcoholism than mainstream adults their age, a sign that no matter how well they speak English, dress for success "a la Americana," or drive a new car (that he or she paid for 100 percent), the stressors and adjustments characteristic of the acculturating Hispanic market are present, and have an impact in their daily lives.

FIGURE 10.1 .. ..

GenAge Segments: Latinos and Latinas, Aged 20 to 39, 2006

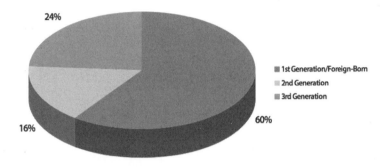

Source: M. Isabel Valdés. The 2006 data is consistent with independent estimates including those from the Pew Hispanic Center and the Census Bureau's 2006 March Current Population Survey, Annual Social and Economic Supplement, ©2007.

FIGURE 10.2 .. .. :. .. ..

GenAge Segments: Latinos and Latinas, Aged 20 to 39, 2006

(in thousands)

TOTAL LATINOS/ LATINAS	1ST GENERATION/ FOREIGN-BORN	U.S.-BORN TOTAL	2ND GENERATION	3RD GENERATION OR GREATER
15,461	9,274	6,187	2,520	3,667
100%	60%	40%	16%	24%

Source: M. Isabel Valdés. The 2006 data is consistent with independent estimates including those from the Pew Hispanic Center and the Census Bureau's 2006 March Current Population Survey, Annual Social and Economic Supplement, © 2007.

They are hard workers, striving to succeed in the U.S. and many more are completing graduate school than previous generations. They are intent on providing for their families by taking advantage of all the United States has to offer while at the same time retaining their strong family and cultural ties. Many work two jobs.

GenAge twenty-something and thirty-something consumers can enjoy a growing number of dedicated media. With more than 15 million consumers and more disposable income than preceding generations, as well as greater acculturation, media companies continue to develop special media vehicles to talk to them directly. Magazines like *Latina, People en Español,* and *Latina Style* spearheaded the trend. Today many TV, radio, and print media are available to target American Latinas and Latinos. In addition, many popular Latin American magazines are being sold in the U.S.

A well-known cultural fact is that Latino families are larger, and the marketing opportunities this represents relates to this market segment. Despite a 19-year age span (20–39) within the segment, these Hispanic consumers have many things in common. For example, both age segments are forming families. The younger group (20–29) is beginning to form families with the birth of their first child, while couples in the older group (30–39) are also having children.

Some Latina moms continue to bear children well over age 40. These later-in-life births are not a new trend among Hispanic women. On the contrary, they follow a social tradition prevalent in many Latin America countries where it is common to find Latin American families where the first grandchild of the family is the same age as the youngest child of the grandparents. The childbearing years of the traditional Hispanic woman are longer than those of the white non-Hispanic woman in the United States. This has far-reaching marketing implications since companies selling diapers and baby food, for example, need to address a wider range of ages and issues than they do in the general market. For other products or service categories such as car insurance, cosmetics, apparel, etc., the broad age range does not make such a difference. Marketers should split the age segment following the specific needs of the category of business.

Twenty-somethings: Aged 20 to 29
Sub-Segment Size: 7.7 million (17 percent)

FIGURE 10.3 . . . .

GenAge Segments: Twenty-somethings, Aged 20 to 29, 2006

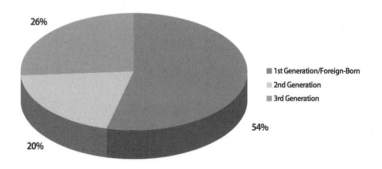

FIGURE 10.4 .. ..

GenAge Segments: Twenty-somethings, Aged 20 to 29, 2006

(in thousands)

TOTAL TWENTY-SOMETHINGS	1ST GENERATION/FOREIGN-BORN	U.S.-BORN TOTAL	2ND GENERATION	3RD GENERATION OR GREATER
7,740	4,201	3,539	1,516	2,023
100%	54%	46%	20%	26%

Source: M. Isabel Valdés. The 2006 data is consistent with independent estimates including those from the Pew Hispanic Center and the Census Bureau's 2006 March Current Population Survey, Annual Social and Economic Supplement, ©2007.

Thirty-somethings: Aged 30 to 39
Sub-Segment Size: 7.7 million (17 percent)

Latinos and Latinas in their thirties make up 17.3 percent of the U.S. Hispanic population. They are 20 percent more likely to be foreign-born than their twenty-something counterparts, as two thirds (66 percent) were born in a foreign country.

FIGURE 10.5 .. ..: .. ..

GenAge Segments: Thirty-somethings, Aged 30 to 39, 2006

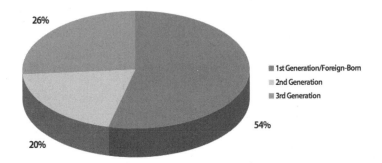

Source: M. Isabel Valdés. The 2006 data is consistent with independent estimates including those from the Pew Hispanic Center and the Census Bureau's 2006 March Current Population Survey, Annual Social and Economic Supplement, © 2007.

FIGURE 10.6 .. ..

GenAge Segments: Thirty-somethings, Aged 30 to 39 , 2006

(in thousands)

TOTAL THIRTY-SOMETHINGS	1ST GENERATION/ FOREIGN-BORN	U.S.-BORN TOTAL	2ND GENERATION	3RD GENERATION OR GREATER
7,719	5,072	2,647	1,003	1,644
100%	66%	34%	13%	21%

Source: M. Isabel Valdés. The 2006 data is consistent with independent estimates including those from the Pew Hispanic Center and the Census Bureau's 2006 March Current Population Survey, Annual Social and Economic Supplement, ©2007.

Latin Boomers: Aged 40 to 59
Segment Size: 9.5 million (21 percent)

Unlike previous generations of 40-to-60-year-old Latinos, the boomers, ÐyoungÐ and ÐmatureÐ Latinos today have improved their incomes and many are becoming active members of the growing Latino middle class, specifically those born in the U.S. Many have seen their dreams come true. An age-standardized study by the Tomás Rivera Policy Institute, released in 2001, estimates that almost 2.7 million Hispanic households had incomes of $40,000 or more. This represents about 40 percent of Latino households, compared with 60 percent of Anglo households that were considered middle class by the same measurement. The group aged 45 to 54, whether foreign or U.S.-born, is most likely of all the age groups to be middle class. Education of U.S.-born Hispanics is helping to raise the number of middle-class households, whereas increased immigration by foreign-born Hispanics is making it more difficult to increase the overall share of Hispanic households that could be considered middle class.

Now in their forties and fifties, Latino boomers were born between the mid-1940s and the mid-1960s. The biggest difference between them and Anglo boomers is that the vast majority (64 percent) were born outside the United States. The younger group (aged 40 to 49) represents 14 percent of total Latinos, and the older group (aged 50 to 59) about 9 percent of the Latino population.

Many of these Hispanic consumers are among the 27 percent of the Hispanic population that entered this country before 1980. They have lived in the United States for about half of their adult lives, and they are likely to have obtained citizenship.

FIGURE 10.7 .. ..

GenAge Segments: Latin Boomers, Aged 40 to 59, 2006

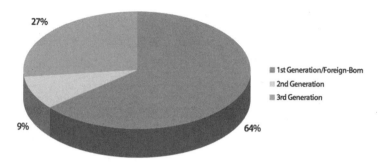

FIGURE 10.8 .. ..

GenAge Segments: Latin Boomers Aged 40 to 59, 2006

(in thousands)

TOTAL BOOMERS	1ST GENERATION/ FOREIGN-BORN	U.S.-BORN TOTAL	2ND GENERATION	3RD GENERATION OR GREATER
9,505	6,103	3,402	883	2,519
100%	64%	36%	9%	27%

Source: M. Isabel Valdés. The 2006 data is consistent with independent estimates including those from the Pew Hispanic Center and the Census Bureau's 2006 March Current Population Survey, Annual Social and Economic Supplement, ©2007.

Young Boomers: Aged 40 to 49
Sub-Segment Size: 5.9 million (13 percent)

FIGURE 10.9 .. ..

GenAge Segments: Young Boomers, Aged 40 to 49, 2006

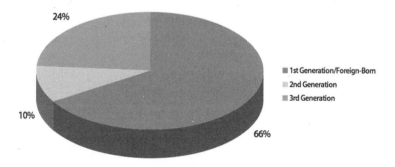

Source: M. Isabel Valdés. The 2006 data is consistent with independent estimates including those from the Pew Hispanic Center and the Census Bureau's 2006 March Current Population Survey, Annual Social and Economic Supplement, ©2007.

| CASESTUDY | WELLPOINT/BLUE CROSS HEALTH INSURANCE |

Campaign: "First Aid"

Agency: cruz/kravetz:IDEAS

The Situation

WellPoint is the nation's largest health insurer, with health plans in 39 states, most under the Blue Cross/Blue Shield name. Blue Cross of California (BCC) is its largest business unit and new product and marketing initiatives are typically tested there prior to national roll-out. BCC had dabbled in Hispanic advertising in the mid 1990s but had abandoned those efforts in the absence of any competitive activity. In 2005, faced with declining enrollment and aggressive competition for Hispanic members from Kaiser and United Health/Pacifi-Care, WellPoint hired **cruz/kravetz:IDEAS** to start over in the Hispanic market.

Consulting

The process began with a thorough assessment of BCC's Hispanic capabilities. The agency devised an Inquire/Buy/Use model to identify all consumer touchpoints. Interviews were scheduled throughout the company to assess its ability to *deliver services* to Latino consumers and to *sell those services* (capture members) to them *before* beginning marketing outreach. The sales process was a particular challenge, requiring significant changes to the call centers.

Research and Strategy

Due to a lack of significant secondary research on Hispanics and health insurance, both qualitative and quantitative research was performed, including in-depth anthropological studies performed at target consumers' homes. The research uncovered significant differences between Latino and general market consumers in terms of the cultural and emotional foundation that defines their relationship with the healthcare system. These differences were largely driven by fatalism, by a past and present-orientation (rather than a forward-thinking perspective) and a tendency to think of healthcare in terms of disease rather than of prevention and well-being. There were also differences in the family's role in healthcare decision making and in their means of accessing health care. One striking result arose from a comparison (using Iconoculture) of Hispanic and general market values related to health care. In this category, Latinos were shown to be more driven by *emotional* values while non-Hispanics were more driven by *rational* values.

It also became clear that Hispanics were not as experienced with how health insurance works and that they would require education on the *value* of having health insurance. A crucial insight was that Latinos saw *life insurance* as an investment on behalf of their

CASESTUDY WELLPOINT/BLUE CROSS HEALTH INSURANCE (CONT.)

children but considered *adult health insurance* as selfish—as something that would consume resources better dedicated to the kids.

A round of message testing helped solidify the communication strategy: *"In insuring myself with BCC, I am a better parent because I am protecting my **kids**' future."*

A parallel process was undertaken to better understand Hispanic small business owners. The research revealed a plethora of misconceptions about employer-provided health insurance. It also showed, consistent with the findings about family insurance, that decisions had a significant emotional component as small business owners tended to develop close personal connections with their employees and had a genuine interest in providing them with peace of mind.

The Campaigns

We launched individual and small business media campaigns in tandem to maximize brand awareness levels. The individual campaign employed television, radio, interactive (including search) and direct mail. The small business campaign employed English-language radio, advertorials in Spanish-language newspapers and bilingual direct mail. Leads were driven to the website and to medium-specific toll free numbers. In addition, we launched an aggressive program of event outreach to Latino business and professional associations.

Results

The advertising was successful in driving leads. In addition, unaided brand awareness increased and advertising awareness tripled from an already substantial "ghost" level.

Hispanic marketing is now seen as the key strategic component in addressing WellPoint's commitment to reducing the number of uninsured in the markets that they serve.

GenAge Segments: Young Boomers, Aged 40-49, 2006

(in thousands)

TOTAL YOUNG BOOMERS	1ST GENERATION/ FOREIGN-BORN	U.S.-BORN TOTAL	2ND GENERATION	3RD GENERATION OR GREATER
5,928	3,905	2,023	572	1,451
100%	66%	34%	10%	24%

Source: M. Isabel Valdés. The 2006 data is consistent with independent estimates including those from the Pew Hispanic Center and the Census Bureau's 2006 March Current Population Survey, Annual Social and Economic Supplement, ©2007.

Mature Boomers : Aged 50 to 59
Sub-Segment Size: 3.6 million (8 percent)

FIGURE 10.11 .. ..

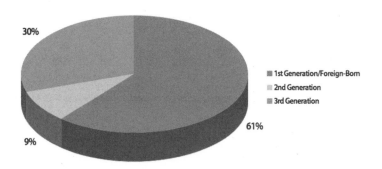

GenAge Segments: Mature Boomers, Aged 50 to 59, 2006

Source: M. Isabel Valdés. The 2006 data is consistent with independent estimates including those from the Pew Hispanic Center and the Census Bureau's 2006 March Current Population Survey, Annual Social and Economic Supplement, ©2007.

FIGURE 10.12 .. ..

GenAge Segments: Mature Boomers Aged 50 to 59, 2006

(in thousands)

TOTAL MATURE BOOMERS	1ST GENERATION/ FOREIGN-BORN	U.S.-BORN TOTAL	2ND GENERATION	3RD GENERATION OR GREATER
3,578	2,198	1,380	312	1,068
100%	61%	39%	9%	30%

Source: M. Isabel Valdés. The 2006 data is consistent with independent estimates including those from the Pew Hispanic Center and the Census Bureau's 2006 March Current Population Survey, Annual Social and Economic Supplement, ©2007.

Marketing to Hispanic Boomer Women

One of the biggest differences between Caucasian and Hispanic boomers in the U.S. is that so many Hispanics of this generation were born outside the U.S. They have emigrated from Mexico, Central and South America, Cuba, and Puerto Rico. They spent their formative years steeped in the highly traditional Latino culture of their countries of origin. On average, they have lived in the U.S. for only half their lives, unlike younger Hispanic generations, who have more fully assimilated into the mainstream American culture and lifestyle.

Hispanic boomers are caught between two cultures, and being older, changes in value systems and lifestyle do not happen easily. For instance, though the "empty nest" phenomenon is challenging and emotionally charged for many boomer moms, it is doubly difficult for the Hispanic mom. Unlike her Anglo-American counterpart, who probably left home for college right after high school, the boomer Hispanic woman was not so independent, remaining at home until marriage. Lacking a similar experience of their own, it is harder to reconcile their children's (especially their daughter's) departure into the world. In fact, it is common to see Hispanic daughters being discouraged from going to college in the most traditional families because it breaks with the cultural model of living at home until marriage.

Latino boomer women tend to put family above all else, sacrificing in the extreme for their kids, parents, and extended relations. This Hispanic woman will respond to messaging, services, and products that speak to her sense of love, care, and duty to keep family bonds strong.

Not surprisingly, Latino boomers are very involved with their grandchildren and aging parents. For Hispanic boomer women, it is a given that every vacation, as long as parents and in-laws are alive, involves multiple generations. They may have to juggle the logistics of caring for aging parents who, in many cases, live outside the United States.

This strong emotional pull of intergenerational family bonds in Latino culture has implications for consumer product marketing as well. Multi-generational communications strategies work especially well with these GenAge segments because they tend not to welcome the concept of experiencing their "golden years" away from their beloved grandchildren and other family members.

I do not imply here that Anglo-American grandmothers do not enjoy close-ness with their grandchildren and family members. However, cross-cultural research shows that the intensity and frequency of contact in Latino families tends to be much greater. It is common for traditional Latino grandparents—particularly those in lower socioeconomic segments—to raise their grandchildren or babysit everyday. Similarly it would be unusual not to have telephone contact everyday, or at least a couple times a week with the nuclear family members.

As an example of a marketing strategy that uses these cultural tendencies, Johnson and Johnson, when developing a new diabetes test kit, took into consideration that Hispanics tend to over index with diabetes (due in large part to their diet). Instead of positioning their message as "do this for yourself," the marketing campaign communicated "address your health issues so you can be there for your kids and grandkids." Appealing to the Latino sense of duty and commitment to family legacy resulted in a very successful campaign.

Marketing to Mature Boomers

There are 6.2 million Latinos over the age of 50 residing in the U.S. today. Until AARP's management decided to target this "maturing" Latino segment, there was no dedicated media or ad campaigns targeting mature Latinos. Two-thirds are foreign-born. Some are now entering their grandparenting years, and others their retirement years. The majority, given the choice, prefers to communicate in Spanish. AARP's *Segunda Juventud* magazine, together with many programs and services they offer, are filling a need in this growing market segment. A detailed case study of AARP's strategy for the Hispanic market, including the organization's initial analysis, campaign, and results, is found in *Marketing to American Latinos: An In-Culture Approach, Part II* (Paramount Market Publishing, 2004).

Los Grandes: Aged 60+
Segment Size: 3.5 million (8 percent)

The total population of the U.S. is aging fast and becoming more multicultural and ethnically diverse. The number of Americans older than age 65 will double over the next 25 years to 70 million, or 20 percent of the population by 2030. In contrast, the Latino population is contributing fewer people to the older age segments, as it is a much younger population overall.

FIGURE 10.13 ....

GenAge Segments: Los Grandes, Aged 60+, 2006

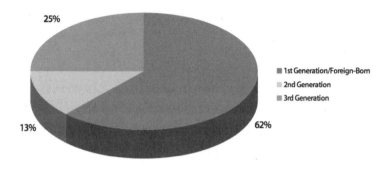

Legend:
- 1st Generation/Foreign-Born
- 2nd Generation
- 3rd Generation

25%
13%
62%

Source: M. Isabel Valdés. The 2006 data is consistent with independent estimates including those from the Pew Hispanic Center and the Census Bureau's 2006 March Current Population Survey, Annual Social and Economic Supplement, ©2007.

Los Grandes, the senior members of the Hispanic market, aged 60 and over in the GenAge Segmentation, represent about 8 percent of all Hispanics. With 62 percent foreign-born, they must "learn the ropes," being both seniors and being seniors in a very different culture.

Usually, seniors' social activities in the traditional Hispanic culture center around the family, and many take care of their grandchildren and other family members. For some of the seniors living in the U.S., that is not the case, as their children and family members live in other cities or are too busy working to visit as often as they would like. Some do live in extended family households and it is estimated that about 11 percent live with their families. Often, if the family lives close by, Los Grandes become surrogate parents while their sons and daughters are studying or at work.

FIGURE 10.14 ....

GenAge Segments: Los Grandes, Aged 60+, 2006

(in thousands)

TOTAL LOS GRANDES	1ST GENERATION/ FOREIGN-BORN	U.S.-BORN TOTAL	2ND GENERATION	3RD GENERATION OR GREATER
3,511	2,181	1,330	440	890
100%	62%	38%	13%	25%

Source: M. Isabel Valdés. The 2006 data is consistent with independent estimates including those from the Pew Hispanic Center and the Census Bureau's 2006 March Current Population Survey, Annual Social and Economic Supplement, ©2007.

Overall, the minority senior population is growing faster than the non-minority population and Hispanics are the fastest growing minority segment in this age group. By 2030, one quarter of the population will be composed of what are now minority groups. The challenge and opportunity created by the multicultural senior population will be huge, impacting health care, consumer products, and all kinds of service industries.

Presently, about 1 million Hispanic households or nearly 11 percent of total Hispanic households are headed by someone aged 65 or older. This share is projected to increase dramatically as the percentage of Hispanics in this age group increases during the coming decades.

The vast majority of Latino seniors have been married at one point in their lives. Among the group aged 65 and older, only 5.7 percent report having never married. By this age, about 62 percent are still married, 11 percent are divorced, and nearly 22 percent are widowed.

Spanish is the only language for the majority, particularly among women. As expected, this has a major impact on these consumers' quality of life, access to information, and so forth. A Southern California study by Latino Health Access with Latinas over age 65 found that 9 out of 10 participants were monolingual Spanish speakers. This limits senior communications and social interactions outside the family and peer groups. The study concluded: "Language barriers may be presumed to restrict access to health care and public services, let alone comprehension of prescription drug inserts or completing applications for various public services." The same report quotes the National Academy on Aging's data, stating, "incomes were lower among older, single Latina women than any other group."

The vast majority of Hispanics in this age group adheres to traditional Hispanic cultural values and do not want to lose the "old ways" of the Hispanic family. Some, particularly the foreign-born who migrated for political or economic reasons, are coping with issues of nostalgia and acculturation. Aging in a different culture is not an easy process for many. For example, many wonder and worry who will take care of them as they age, especially if they do not have a personal pension, a personal support network, and no family lives nearby.

According to the Bureau of the Census, only about 21 percent of Hispanic men and 23 percent of Hispanic women aged 65 and older had a pension in 1998. Unfortunately, Hispanics have less affluence and education as the group gets older. A 2001 study by The Media Audit with almost 10,000 Hispanics shows that only 4.6 percent of Latinos older than age 50 have annual incomes of $50,000 or more. In contrast, 14.3 percent among non-Hispanic whites and 7.3 percent among African-Americans in that age group have incomes of more than $50,000.

Health-wise, Hispanic seniors tend to present a sad picture. Preventive health care is not presently a part of Hispanic culture, as fatalism—"It is the will of God"—tends to be the norm. Many of the present health conditions could be improved drastically with healthcare education and preventive checkups. Corporate America could extend its programs to Los Grandes as a part of its community marketing initiatives. As with the younger age segments, this is an opportunity to build Share of Heart with the Hispanic community.

It is important to underscore, though, that not all Hispanic seniors are poor, nor are they all Spanish-monoligual. However, the lower-income group tends to be over-represented in large urban areas and any program for targeting Los Grandes needs to consider these socioeconomic realities.

The Los Grandes Mindset

Sixty-four percent of Los Grandes are foreign-born and most migrated to the United States as adults. The presence of older Hispanics varies considerably by market. For example, Cubans in Miami are over-represented in this age group, whereas in Los Angeles, Cubans are under-represented.

As in the general market, the Latino senior market segment is divided into two distinct age sub-groups that have quite different needs and realities. The "young senior" segment is aged 60 to 69, and the "senior senior" group is aged 70 and older. Because women tend to live longer than men, the share of Latina seniors in this segment increases with age.

Like most seniors today, Latino seniors are caught between generations, and, as previously mentioned, they have to live between different and sometimes conflicting cultural values. They are caught between their personal aging and health needs, the needs of their children and grandchildren, and occasionally even the needs of their own aging parents—"Triple Decker," or "Sandwich Generation" households. According to AARP, far more Latinos tend to feel sandwiched between generations compared with other cultural groups.

For example, cultural differences between seniors and their more Americanized family members in daily or weekly interaction with *el abuelito* (grandpa) or *la abuelita* (grandma) can be a challenge. The younger generation's perspective and world views sometimes disagree with the senior's "non-acculturated" perspective. This often creates emotional gaps. On the other hand, more accul- turated family members can provide seniors with the help, degree of comfort, and support they need. As a matter of fact, the family, when available, can be a great help in communicating with or marketing to Latino seniors.

Marketing to Los Grandes In-Culture

The need for Latino senior marketing is being recognized. For example, a special program has been announced by Pfizer to reduce the cost of drugs for low-income people. This brings Pfizer to the forefront of Latino Share of Heart while building brand recognition. It not only captures seniors' attention with a positive spin but the attention of their families as well, building loyalty within the entire Hispanic community. We all notice when a company does something special to help those in need.

The suggestions that follow can help make sure your Latino senior marketing program is on target.

- As most are foreign-born, assume many Latino seniors will have little or no knowledge of the basics of your program, service, or product. These need to be explained in clear, basic terms.

- Assume most have vision problems—print must be large and clear.

- Use simple sentences; repeat key points of the message in user-friendly formats.

- Good and basic Spanish is essential. Bilingual communication is recommended to reach seniors and their caretakers.

- Low literacy is an issue with Los Grandes. Therefore, consider visual communications with verbal explanations (photographs, videos, radio, and toll-free numbers manned by Spanish-speaking operators). Distrust of government organizations and small legal print is common.

- Include the family, the adult children, and grandchildren whenever possible, either in the promotions (e.g., "ask your family") or in the actual programs, if applicable. Communications messages should show the grandparent at the table with the grandchild, or going to the theatre with another family member.

- Repeat and communicate slowly in a pace that feels relaxed and joyful.

- Show uplifting, smiling faces in visuals, ads, and TV commercials.

- When developing Hispanic senior communications strategies or campaigns, include caretakers in the research. They will act as gatekeepers.

- Always show respect. Use the more formal, traditional communications approach.

- Test for linguistic barriers. Depending on country of origin, some words will not be known to all. Make it as easy as possible.

- Don't expect seniors to look for your telephone number. Provide it.

- Traditional Hispanic social customs, Familismo, are religious traditions and values must be considered and used whenever possible.

- Senior Latino children are many times the "official" shoppers, caretakers, or "managers" for their parents. Hence, the strategic analysis has to determine if the primary target is the senior, the caretaker-children, or both.

- To reach seniors and their caretakers, campaigns need to integrate mass media with community organizations. They need to support print and new electronic media as well. Latino seniors, some more than others, are highly skeptical and often reluctant to try new services, go to unknown places, or use unknown brands or products. They will prefer to wait and see how others like a new product or service before trying it themselves. Therefore, additional time needs to be included in the marketing process to allow the social-network, word-of-mouth communications systems to work.

Getting Older—Younger

A small segment of Los Grandes follows a similar pattern of the general population "age compression phenomenon"; that is, older consumers who behave, feel, and live as younger people more so than any other senior consumer group before them. This small Latino segment will most probably grow significantly as the Latino/Latina segments reach middle age. Presently, little is known beyond the author's qualitative measurement. However, based on the present financial and educational gains of younger Hispanics, it can be guessed that the "younger" seniors and senoras are more acculturated and professional, and have more education, higher incomes, and are bilingual or English monolingual.

CHAPTER 11

Making a Marketing Choice Based on Acculturation

The Hispanic market is a "moving target." Just when marketers think they have figured out how to market to Hispanics successfully, major socio-demographic shifts take place, changing the rules of the game. Hand-in-hand with the socio-demographic shifts, the acculturation process continues its inexorable impact on the market, particularly with the younger generations and the growing numbers of foreign-born Latinos who have become more acculturated while living twenty or thirty years in the United States.

As complex as this already is, it gets more complicated. Brand new immigrants are added to the on-going migration of Latinos who join family members or are in search of better living conditions. In addition to the non-acculturated Latinos, there also are Latino consumers who may never acculturate, increasing the demand for Spanish-language media and creative strategies that need to include basic, introductory messages if your strategy calls for a total Hispanic market connection. In other words, the whole spectrum of the acculturation continuum is present in the Hispanic marketplace. What changes is the size of the acculturated versus non-acculturated Hispanic segments.

In my experience, the way to approach the growth opportunity is to execute an in-culture approach to the business plan, the marketing and advertising strategies, and retail. This will prevent you from missing a cultural detail that can derail your investment and ROI.

In this final chapter, I am using a case study to show, in practical terms, how the theory and data presented throughout the book are used in-culture. The in-culture marketing methodology is an all-inclusive, "holistic" approach to consumers that incorporates not only their culture (values orientation, hope, dreams, wants, likes and dislikes) and purchase behavior but also everything that surrounds them—their lifestyles, work, their social networks, and everyday life! For example, the family, the central pillar of the traditional Hispanic culture, includes nuclear as well as extended family members. Everything that takes place in their daily lives as they learn to succeed and adapt to their new host country is fertile ground for creative strategy development. Humor is especially important.

Understanding of the differences in acculturation level of the family group can open doors to situations that can be seminal to the creative and marketing strategies.

I am highly indebted to Frito-Lay for their generous contribution to this and previous book, particularly to Charlie Veraza, vice president, marketing, Frito-Lay North America, and his team, as well as their Hispanic advertising agency, Dieste, Harmel and Partners (San Antonio, Texas) who executed the ad campaign.

CASESTUDY   LAY'S HISPANIC SUNFLOWERS INITIATIVE 2007

Background

As part of Frito-Lay's ongoing corporate commitment to make each of its products more healthy, the Lay's brand began cooking the product in 100 percent pure sunflower oil in late 2006. The resulting consumer benefit of this change in oil is the reduction of saturated fat by at least 50 percent versus previous Lay's potato chips (which were made with a blend of cottonseed, sunflower and corn oil).

Consumer testing showed that communicating this change could be effective in getting consumers to lower health-related consumption barriers to the product, and to feel better about eating Lay's.

With regards to sales, 60 percent of total brand sales are in the top 10 Hispanic markets while 50 percent of total brand sales are in Mexican Hispanic markets. Driven by flavors (e.g., Limón, Chile Limón) and Better for You products (e.g., Lay's Baked, Lay's Light), sales for the brand were up 10 percent in 2006 compared with 2005.

Previous Hispanic initiatives for the brand have focused almost entirely on television, with no supporting in-store activities. The goal of the 2007 Hispanic Lay's initiative was to develop a 360-degree program that would surround consumers with a symphony of communication at every opportunity throughout the day.

With the launch of the sunflower oil initiative in late 2006, the brand also began taking price gains for the first time in several years in an effort to boost profitability. As such, a key objective for the program was to minimize the anticipated sales declines that would result from the price gains.

| CASESTUDY | LAY'S HISPANIC SUNFLOWERS INITIATIVE 2007 (CONT.) |

Marketing Challenge

Historically, the Lay's brand had developed initiatives for the Hispanic market which were distinct from General Market activities. For example, in 2006, General Market communications focused on driving consumption frequency with consumers by communicating around a common occasion, eating Lay's with a sandwich.

However, in the Spanish-language market, sandwich consumption is not as relevant as in the General Market, so that message wouldn't have been as compelling. Instead, the brand focused the Hispanic strategy on building penetration for a Latin-inspired flavor, Chile Limon.

The brand wanted to leverage one message (Sunflower) across all consumer targets to achieve maximum awareness and consistency of the new communication.

The challenge with the 2007 Lay's Sunflower project was to launch the sunflower communication and its corresponding consumer benefit (50 percent less saturated fat) in a way that was, first, relevant for the Spanish-language-dominant consumer, second, consistent with the fun and all-family tonality of the brand, and third, appealing to the young, "more acculturated" family members.

Before the communication plan could take shape though, it first became necessary to confirm that sunflowers had the same positive imagery among Hispanic consumers that they do for General Market consumers. This confirmation was achieved by qualitatively sampling a cross-section of Hispanic consumers through consumer intercepts. More specifically, it was found that "sunflowers" as a visual icon, evoke a happy, tranquil, almost spiritual imagery. In addition, though the benefits of sunflower oil were not definitively known, it was perceived to be healthy.

More formalized focus groups substantiated the findings of these initial consumer intercepts. As part of the focus group research, benefit statements were put in front of consumers to gauge their receptiveness to the sunflower message. Expanding upon the intercept findings, the focus groups confirmed that the Lay's Sunflower message (balanced with taste reassurance) represented a solid opportunity to increase frequency among the target Hispanic audience by substituting for other competitive potato chip brands.

Campaign Objectives

- Achieve brand sales of 90 percent versus YAG. (Note: This objective is based on the significant price gains that were taken on the brand in 2007 to elevate brand profitability.)

CASESTUDY   LAY'S HISPANIC SUNFLOWERS INITIATIVE 2007 (CONT.)

- Increase Hispanic consumers' emotional connection to the brand via breakthrough advertising concept.
- Elevate the brand's health and wellness credentials among Hispanic consumers.

Target Audience

Primary Target: Unacculturated, HispanicWomen, aged 18 to 49;

Secondary Target: Their children and family members

- 54 percent say their number one concern about health risks is "being overweight."
- 58 percent say their number one concern about the food eaten is fat content.
- They express feeling a pang of guilt, especially when giving Lay's to children.
  - "If my kids ask for them, I buy them. But I don't buy a big bag. They have a lot of fat."
  - "I'd limit intake of chips because of the cholesterol, diabetes, and bad nutrition."
  - "Chips have a lot of fat and cholesterol."
- Represent a fast-growing segment.
  - Younger, larger family size.
  - Two-thirds are Mexican and live mostly in West, Southwest, and Chicago.
  - Remaining one-third are primarily Caribbean and live in key competitive potato chips markets like New York City.
  - Main decision-makers for family purchases
- 25 percent are unacculturated Hispanics.
  - Most comfortable speaking Spanish.
  - Positive attitudes about advertising.
  - Influencers of children's behavior changes
- Consume lots of media, but also love in-store promotions.
  - Trade promotions very efficient and effective in Hispanic stores.

Creative Strategy

The creative strategy for the Lay's Hispanic Sunflower Initiative was to get the target audience to **"feel good"** about serving Lay's potato chips to their children, friends and family by telling them that the new Lay's has the same great taste, but with at least half the saturated fat as previous Lay's potato chips, because Lay's is now made with 100 percent Pure Sunflower oil.

CASESTUDY LAY'S HISPANIC SUNFLOWERS INITIATIVE 2007 (CONT.)

This strategy was delivered to the consumer via a two-pronged approach. The first included the adaptation of a 30-second General Spot entitled "A Place in the Sun." The spot was highlighted by an abundance of sunflower imagery to help establish the naturalness of the product with high-energy vignettes to position the brand around the concept of **joy**. In addition, copy highlighted that Lay's is made with "100% Pure Sunflower Oil" and "Half the Saturated Fat." The spot ends with the Lay's Sunflower logo set against a blue sky.

This spot aired in the beginning of the campaign in January 2007 to compliment the General Market message and to launch the new product news in the Hispanic market that Lay's is now made with 100 percent pure sunflower oil.

The tagline featured in the logo lockup was **"La Felicidad Perfecta"** (Perfect Happiness). The tagline was a transliteration of the General Market tagline of "100% Pure Joy." "La Felicidad Perfecta" was chosen as the tagline because "joy" relates to many things in Spanish. As is used in the case of the advertising campaign, "felicidad" ("happiness") was chosen as the most accurate translation of the type of joy being expressed in the campaign. In addition, rather than just translating "100% Pure" more literally ("Cien por Ciento"), **"Perfecta"** was chosen because of its friendlier, more conversational tone and manner.

This strategy was brought to life by depicting small, culturally-relevant annoyances that were made tolerable because the hero in the spot had Lay's potato chips. Two TV spots were created to deliver this message, "Latin Heat" and "Honking Horn."

CASESTUDY   LAY'S HISPANIC SUNFLOWERS INITIATIVE 2007 (CONT.)

The "Latin Heat" spot features Alfonso Posada, who one day lost his Latin blood in a blood transfusion. Even so, Alfonso was happy because he had Lay's.

Four vignettes in the spot featured Alfonso greeted by looks of disbelief and polite coughs at the family dinner table, a concerned look from his grandmother while driving in the car to polka music, awkward (decidedly non-Latino) dance moves at a salsa club, and correcting a bank teller on the pronunciation of his last name by telling him "It's Po-sA-da."

The "Honking Horn" spot features Matias, whose horn (which plays "La Cucaracha") got stuck one day. As with Alfonso, Matias is still happy despite this annoyance because he has Lay's.

LEFT: ALFONSO IN
"LATIN HEAT"
RIGHT: MATIAS
IN "HONKING
HORN"

Four vignettes feature Matias driving by two Mexican males on the sidewalk who mistake Matias' horn as their cell phone ring, followed by Matias driving through the carwash with the drowning sound of his still stuck car horn, to chasing away annoyed movie goers at a drive-in movie theatre, to greeting his neighbor the following morning with his still stuck (though dying with a low battery) car horn.

Both Alfonso and Matias are depicted in the spots as real, authentic people who are choosing to have a good attitude and "perfect happiness" despite their annoying circumstances.

The "Latin Heat" and "Honking Horn" spots end by depicting the hero of the spot within the center of a sunflower, transforming to a field of sunflowers with the sun above transforming to the Lay's Sunflower logo and the tagline "La Felicidad Perfecta" (Perfect Happiness). The humor appeals to all family members, young – and young at heart!

A 30-sheet and bus shelter out-of-home (OOH) campaign supported the television spots. This campaign featured a member of the target audience with an annoyance in the first photo that, despite the annoyance, was happy because he or she had a bag of Lay's in the second photo. A sunflower and the "La Felicidad Perfecta" tagline separated the two photos. As with the TV spots, the OOH executions feature real people with a positive attitude and "perfect happiness" despite their circumstances.

Media Strategy

The media strategy was built on using network TV as the main reach vehicle for the target to gain awareness of the "100% pure sunflower oil" message. A heavy mix of the primetime daypart was scheduled to deliver the greatest reach among Hispanic gatekeeper moms.

The flighting strategy called for a launch with heavy media weight to establish strong initial reach, syncing with the General Marketing flighting where appropriate. Following the launch, the TV flighting was condensed to run Wednesday through Sunday to capitalize on weekend shopping, putting the message closest to the moment of consumer purchase.

The daypart mix mirrored the target's watching habits and included Day (10 percent), Fringe (10 percent), Primetime (55 percent), Sports (10 percent), Late Night (5 percent) and Weekend (10 percent).This daypart mix was supported by three tiers of programming. The first tier, Sponsorships, included **Premio lo Nuestro.**

The sponsorship for Premio lo Nuestro included a schedule of thirty-second Lay's spots married to 30-second Univision-produced vignettes that highlighted Lay's sponsorship of Premio lo Nuestro. These sponsorship spots aired two weeks prior to Premio lo Nuestro. The actual program itself included two thirty-second spots, in which "Latin Heat" and "Honking Horn" were aired. Overall, Premio lo Nuestro was included in the media buy to build rapid reach of the sunflower message and to leverage the captured audience pulled in by what is typically the highest-rated annual program on Spanish-language television.

The second programming tier was broad reach drivers, which included novelas, sports recap shows (to bring in the male demographic), game shows, variety shows, and morning talk shows. The third tier included programming which encompassed the essence of joy. These programs included family-oriented shows, comedies, and movies.

The overall delivery of the media plan (TV only) was a 64 percent reach (55 percent 3+ Effective Reach) with a 12.9 frequency. In the markets with outdoor advertising, the delivery was a 90 percent reach with an 8.9 frequency.

In addition to network television, a 50 showing of 30-Sheet and Bus Shelter advertising was scheduled in each of five markets to increase reach by taking the message to light TV viewers. As well, 30-sheet and bus shelter advertising were included in the media plan to reach consumers in the retail channel.

Two criteria were used to determine the markets for outdoor advertising. First, high-density Hispanic markets were cross-referenced with top Lay's sales markets to narrow the selection. Once this list was established, selecting only those markets that had a high

CASESTUDY   LAY'S HISPANIC SUNFLOWERS INITIATIVE 2007 (CONT.)

composition of the target audience further narrowed the markets. The resulting markets selected through this process were Los Angeles, New York, Miami, Phoenix and Chicago.

Lastly, non-traditional OOH elements were scheduled to create consumer buzz while strengthening the brand positioning around the concept of joy.

Other Supporting "Fun" Programs

In addition to the traditional communication elements, the Lay's Hispanic Sunflower initiative included two unique elements. The first of which was a sound-activated device at retail that was accompanied by a floor graphic. The floor graphic was the Lay's sunflower logo with "La Felicidad Perfecta" (Perfect Happiness) tagline. When consumers passed by the Lay's chips in Hispanic-targeted stores, they were greeted with one of three complimentary messages that included a typical Latin American behavior, **a flirtatious and complimentary whistle.**

The second non-traditional element was a sunflower mirror. These mirrors were placed at locations including subways and bus stops. In the center of the flower was a mirror. While looking in the mirror, consumers would notice an uplifting message on one of the petals to the left of the mirror. An example of the message was: **"Some people wait years to be happy. You already look happy, and your bus won't be long."**

LEFT: SUNFLOWER
MIRROR
RIGHT: FLOOR
GRAPHIC

Results

- Despite significant price gains taken on the brand in 2007, the Lay's Hispanic Sunflower initiative lifted sales above the stated objective and General Market performance when the campaign went on air (see charts below). Results for the launch of the Hispanic initiative were as follows.

- Lay's Hispanic sales were up 103 percent vs. YA (source: IRI).

- Lay's Hispanic sales were up a full 6 points above General Market results (source: IRI).

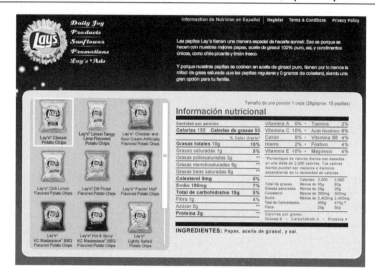

LAY'S WEBSITE

- Post-production focus groups confirmed the breakthrough potential of the "Latin Heat" and "Honking Horn" TV spots. (source: *Multicultural Insights*, 2007).

  – "In all three groups, the Lay's commercial, 'Latin Heat', clearly had 'break-through,' generated laughter and conversation, and was deemed by a majority of the women to be a commercial they *would* watch. Respondents almost unanimously agreed that this commercial was more memorable and entertaining than other ads for salty snacks."

  – "The group described 'Honking Horn' as 'attention-getting,' 'very different,' 'funny,' 'entertaining,' 'informative,' and as a commercial which did inspire them to want Lay's."

Directory of Online Resources

Author's Note The directory no doubt omits some websites. if you would like to have your website listed in subsequent printings, send your url to ivc@isabelvaldes.com, and I will gladly include it.

SEGMENT	SITE	TARGET AUDIENCE
Especially for Latinas		
Chicanas	www.chicanas.com	women
De mujer.com	www.demujer.com	portal for women
Latin Girl Magazine	www.latingirlmag.com	magazine for teens
MANA	www.hermana.org	national Latina organization
Education		
Hispanic Association of Colleges and Universities	www.hacu.net	post-secondary education access for Latinos
Hispanic College Fund	www.hispanicfund.org	funds, grants and scholarships
Hispanic Link	www.hispaniclink.org	internships and scholarships for Hispanics in media
Hispanic Scholarship Fund	www.hsf.net	scholarships and grants
LAMP: Latinos and Media Project	www.latinosandmedia.org	University of Texas at Austin
Latin American Educational Foundation	www.laef.org	higher education
Latin American Network Info Center	www.lanic.utexas.edu	University of Texas at Austin
Advocacy Organizations		
Annie E. Casey Foundation	www.aecf.org	children's advocacy
Association of Hispanic Arts	www.latinoarts.org	media advocacy
Congressional Hispanic Caucus Institute	www.chci.org	political advocacy
Hispanas Organized for Political Equality	www.latinas.org	political advocacy
Hispanics Across America	www.haamerica.org	community advocacy
Hispanic Association on Corporate Responsibility	www.hacr.org	advocacy with corporations
Hispanic Scholarship Fund	www.hsf.net	education funds
Hispanos Famosos	coloquio.com	information about famous Hispanics
Labor Council for Latin American Advancement	www.lclaa.org	trade union association

SEGMENT	SITE	TARGET AUDIENCE
Business and Financial		
Aviso	www.aviso.net/usa/hispanic	Hispanic business directory
Business News Americas	www.bnamericas.com	business news
Dr.Tango	www.drtango.com	online content and applications consulting for healthcare companies
Greater Washington Ibero-American Chamber of Commerce	www.iberochamber.org	Washington, D.C., area Hispanic Chamber of Commerce
Hispanic Business	www.hispanicbusiness.com	magazine and research on line primarily on business news
Hispanic Business Women's Alliance	www.hbwa.net	Hispanic business women's organization
Hispanic-Market	www.hispanic-market.com	business in Hispanic market
Hispanic Network Magazine	www.hnmagazine.com	business and employment opportunities
Latin American Newsletter	www.latinnews.com	Latin American business news
Latin Business Association	www.lbausa.com	business Association
Latin Chamber of Commerce of USA	www.camacol.org	Hispanic Chamber of Commerce in Florida
Latin Trade	www.latintrade.com	Latin Trade magazine's online presence
Mundo Latino	www.MundoLatino.com	business news weekly
US Hispanic Chamber of Commerce	www.ushcc.com	Equivalent of U.S. Chamber of Commerce for Hispanic businesses
US-Mexico Chamber of Commerce	www.usmcoc.org	organization promoting business between the U.S. and Mexico
Viajo.com	www.viajo.com	business & leisure
Zona Financiera	www.zonafinanciera.com	Latin America finance
E-Commerce		
El Coqui Gifts	www.elcoquigifts.com	gifts
Espanol.com	www.espanol.com	e-commerce
Mercado Libre	www.MercadoLibre.com	e-commerce
The Human Bean	www.thehumanbean.com	Zapatista coffee from Chaipas Mexico plus politics
Todito.com	www.todito.com	e-commerce
Entertainment and Film		
Cine Las Americas	www.cinelasamericas.org	film
Cinemaluna	www.cinemaluna.com	film
CineSol Latino Film Festival	www.cinesol.com	film
Es Mas	www.esmas.com	entertainment
Galan Incorporated Television and Film	www.galaninc.com	film
Latino Film Festival	www.latinofilmfestival.org	film

SEGMENT	SITE	TARGET AUDIENCE
Entertainment and Film (cont.)		
Latino Issues Forum	www.lif.org	advocacy organization
League of United Latin American Citizens	www.lulac.org	advocacy organization
Lee Seràs	www.leeseras.net	literacy organization
Mexican-American Legal Defense and Educational Fund	www.maldef.org	Mexican American legal defense and education
National Association for Bilingual Education	www.nabe.org	advocacy for language-minority students
National Council of La Raza	www.nclr.org	advocacy for low-income Hispanics
National Hispanic Foundation for the Arts	www.hispanicarts.org	media advocacy organization
National Latino Children's Institute	www.nosotros.org	advocacy for Latino children
Nosotoros	www.nosotros.org	advocacy organization for Latino performers
National Association of Hispanic Publications	www.nahp.org	advocacy organization representing Hispanic publications
The Latino Coalition	www.thelatinocoalition.com	political advocacy
Arts and Culture		
Arte Publico Press	www.arte.uh.edu	literature
Bilingual Foundation of the Arts	www.bfatheatre.org	Hispanic world drama
Frida Kahlo	www.fridakahlo.com	art
Global Music Directory	www.dgolpe.com	music
Hispanic Art	www.arteamericas.com	art
Hispanic Society of America	www.hispanicsociety.org	culture
Hispano Mundo	www.Hispanomundo.com	history and culture
Joe Villarreal Art Gallery	www.joevartist.com	art
La Musica	www.lamusica.com	music
Mexican Museum	www.mexicanmuseum.org	museum
Museo de la Americas	www.museo.org	museum
Museo de barrio	www.elmuseo.org	museum
National Hispanic Cultural Center Foundation	www.hcfoundation.org	Hispanic arts and humanities
Smithsonian Center for Latin Initiatives	Latino.si.edu	information on and photos of exhibits, job opportunities, research all for Latinos
Somos Primos	www.somosprimos.com	Hispanic heritage and history
The Library of Congress Hispanic Reading Room	www.loc.gov/rr/hispanic	What the Library of Congress offers on Hispanic and Latin America art
Virtual Diego Rivera Web Museum	www.diegorivera.com	information on and photos of exhibits

SEGMENT	SITE	TARGET AUDIENCE
Arts and Culture (cont.)		
Los Angeles Latino International Film Festival	www.latinofilm.org	film
Miami Latin Film Festival	www.hispanicfilm.com	film
National Alliance for Media Arts and Culture	www.namac.org	film
New York International Latino Film Festival	www.nylatinofilm.com	film
San Diego Latino Film Festival	www.sdlatinofilm.com	film
Tulipanes Latino Art & Film Festival	www.tlaff.org	film
Vivahollywood.com	www.vivahollywood.com	entertainment
LatinBayArea	www.latinbayarea.com	entertainment
Health		
Buena Salud	www.buenasalud.com	health information for Spanish-speakers
Hispanic Health	www.hispanichealth.org	health information and advocacy
Office of Minority Health Resources Center	www.omhrc.gov	links to health services for Hispanics; listings by state
SAMHSA	wwww.health.org	clearinghouse for alcohol and drug information
Todo Bebé	www.todobebe.com	Infant care and parenting
Job Search		
Bilingual Jobs	www.Bilingual-Jobs.com	job search
Hire Diversity	www.hirediversity.com	recruitment
Hispanic Employment Program	www.helpm.org	job search
iHispano	www.ihispano.com	job search
Job Latino	www.joblatino.com	job search
Lat Pro	www.LatPro.com	job search
Monster.com Espanol	espanol.monster.com	Job search
Saludos	www.saludos.com	job search
U.S. Navy	www.elnavy.com	recruitment
Literature		
Criticas magazine	www.crtiticas.com	reviews in Spanish of Spanish-language books
Hispanic Culture Review	www.gmu.edu/org/hcr	journal published by students of George Mason University poetry and stories
Isabel Allende	www.isabelallende.com	literature
Libros Latinos	www.libroslatinos.com	literature
Nuestra Palabra	www.nuestrapalabra.org	literature

SEGMENT	SITE	TARGET AUDIENCE
Marketing, Market Research, and Advertising		
Ads Media	www.adsmediagroup.com	direct media
Allied Media	www.allied-media.com	multi-cultural advertising and marketing
Cheskin	www.cheskin.com	market research company
Cultural Access Group	www.accesscag.com	market research company
Echo Media	www.ech_media.com	direct media
HispanicAd.com	www.hispanicad.com	advertising and media news and information
Hispanic Digital Network	www.hdnweb.com	advertising and design services
Hispanicity	www.hispanicity.com	Hispanic advertising and marketing
Hispanic PR Wire	www.hispanicprwire.com	Hispanic news and PR distribution
Hispanic-Research Co.	www.hispanic-research.com	marketing consultants
Informania.com	www.informania.com	Subscriptions available in Spanish. Information on the internet economy, bilingual dictionary, resource center
Isabel Valdés	www.isabelvaldes.com	marketing consulting
La fuente de Informacion de la prensa Hispana	www.hispanic-media.com	information and analysis about Hispanic media
Latin American Research Group of the Federal Reserve Bank	www.frbatlanta.org/econ_rd/larg	finance and economic research in Latin America
Latina Force, Inc.	www.latinaforce.com	lists and maps for multicultural direct marketing
LatinPak	www.latinapak.com	direct marketing
Latin Vision	www.latinvision.com	marketing consultants
Media Economics Group	www.Latinwebmonitor.com	monitors advertising spending on Hispanic web-sites
Media Economics Group	www.hispanicmagazine monitor.com	monitors advertising spending on Hispanic print market
Multicultural Marketing Resources		marketing resource for marketing executives and journalists.
National Association of Hispanic Media	www.nahp.org	media kit
Pew Hispanic Center	www.pewhispanic.org	publishes excellent analysis of Hispanic data as well as original survey work
Roslow Research Group	www.roslowresearch.com	market research company
Santiago Solutions Group	www.santiagosolutions group.com	marketing consultants
Selig Center	www.selig.uga.edu	economic studies of multicultural markets
SRDS	www.srds.com	publishers of *Hispanic Media & Market Source*
Strategy Research	www.strategyresearch.com	marketing consultants

SEGMENT	SITE	TARGET AUDIENCE
Media		
The Tomás Rivera Policy Institute	www.trpi.org	publishes research on the Hispanic population in the U.S., excellent research on the Hispanic middle class among other things
Annuario Hispano	www.hispanicyearbook.com	excellent directory of Hispanic radio and TV stations,
Batanga	www.batanga.com	internet radio and other services
CNN en Espanol	www.cnnenespanol.com	news
Contacto Magazine	www.contactomagazine.com	news magazine
Dos Mundos	www.dosmundos.com	bilingual newspaper from Kansas City
El Conquistador	www.conquistadornewspaper.com	newspaper
El Extra News	www.extranews.com	newspaper
El Heraldo	www.elheraldo.com	newspaper
El Hood	www.elhood.com	music and entertainment website
El Nuevo Herald	www.miami.com/elnuevoherald	newspaper
El Sol de Texas	www.elsoldetexas.com	newspaper
Enlance	www.enlancelink.com	news in Spanish
Fox Sports en Espanol	msn.foxsports.com/fse	sports in Spanish
Galavision	www.galavision.com	television network
Hawaii Hispanic News	www.hawaiihispanicnews.com	newspaper from Hawaii
Hispanic Online	www.hispaniconline.com	*Hispanic Magazine* website
Hola	www.hola.com	celebrity news magazine
Impremedia	www.impremedia.com	Spanish language newspaper
La Conexion	www.LaConexionUSA.com	newspaper—North Carolina
La Oferta	www.laoferta.com	newspaper
La Opinión	www.laopinion.com	newspaper in Spanish—Los Angeles
La Prensa San Diego	www.laprensa-sandiego.org	bilingual newspaper—San Diego
La Raza	www.laraza.com	Spanish language newspaper—Chicago
LA Ritmo	www.laritmo.com	Latin American rhythm magazine in English
Latina	www.latina.com	magazine for women
Latina Style	www.latinastyle.com	fashion magazine for women
Latino News Network	www.latnn.com	website
LA TV	www.latv.com	Los Angeles-based music and entertainment channel

SEGMENT	SITE	TARGET AUDIENCE
Media (cont.)		
Noticias Wire	www.noticiaswire.com	Hispanic internet newswire
People en Espanol	www.peopleenespanol.com	Spanish edition of *People* magazine
qvMagazine	www.qvmagazine.com	magazine for gay Latino men
Sitv	www.sitv.com	English language TV for Latinos in Los Angeles
Telemundo	www.telemundo.com	television network
TV Azteca	www.tvazteca.com.mx	Mexican television network
Univision	www.univision.com	television network
Urban Latino	www.urbanlatino.com	magazine
V Me	www.v-me.tv	Spanish public television
Zona Latina	www.zonalatina.com	links to Latin American media
Online Community		
Spanish Pride	www.spanishpride.com	Spanish and English: pen pals, message board, games, shopping, music
Portals		
Asociados	www.Asociados.com	general
El Sitio	www.Elsitio.com	general
Es Mas	www.Esmas.com	general
Hispanic	www.hispanic.com	general
Hispanic Vista	www.hispanicvista.com	general
Latino	www.latino.com	general
Latino LA	www.latinola.com	Los Angeles Latinos
LatinoWeb	www.latinos.com	general
MSN Latino	latino.msn.com	general
Quepasa	www.quepasa.com	general
Starmedia	www.starmedia.com	general
Terra	www.terra.com	general
Telemundo/Yahoo en Espanol	www.telemundo.com	general
Yupi/MSN	www.yupimsn.com	general
Hogarlatino	www.hogarlatino.com	general
Hispanicmpr	www.hispanicmpr.com	general
AOL Latino	latino.aol.com	general
Univision	www.univision.com	general
Miscellaneous		
Amtrak Espanol	espanol.amtrak.com	transportation
Auto Mundo Productions, Inc.	www.automundo.com	automotive
HispanicTrends	www.hispanictrends.com	business tends for the Hispanic market
Hispanicvista	www.hispanicvista.com	general

SEGMENT	SITE	TARGET AUDIENCE
Miscellaneous (cont.)		
Portada	www.portada-online.com	Hispanic advertising and publishing news
Ethnicmarketingsolutions	www.ethnicmarketingsolutions.com	marketing company for different ethnic groups
Demarasuhogar	www.delmarasuhogar.com	website of fine seafood products
ContextoLatino	www.contextolatina.com	national Hispanic, editorial features service
Cityreachlatino	www.cityreach_latino.com	Hispanic media
LatinClips	www.latinclips.com	Hispanic clipping services
Latinheat	www.latinheat.com	English language publication and website focusing on Latinos in the entertainment industry
Laantidroga	www.antridroga.com	drug prevention program in Leangles
Edexcelencia	www.edexcelencia.org	examples of excellence in education
Estradausa	www.estradausa.com	U.S. Hispanic consumer market & Latino community issues
Despegar	www.despegar.com	online travel
LatinoUSA	www.latinousa	radio journal of news and culture produced from a Latino perspective
LasCulturas	www.lasculturas.com	promoting latino culture
Latinosportslegends.com	www.latinosportslegends.com	all about the sports legends of Latin America
NeighborWorks America	www.nw.org	community building
Peruvianconnection	www.peruvianconnection.com	Peruvian products catalog
Professional Organizations		
American Association of Hispanic CPAs	www.aahcpa.org	Hispanic CPAs
Association of Hispanic Advertising Agencies	www.ahaa.org	Hispanic advertising agencies
Association of Latino Professionals in Finance and Accounting	www.alpfa.com	accounting and finance professionals
California Chicano News Media Association	www.ccnma.org	advocacy for Latino journalists and diversity in the news media
Hispanic National Bar Association	www.hnbar.com	national association for Hispanic lawyers
Hola! Hispanic Organization of Latin Actors	www.hellohola.org	organization for Latino actors
Latin Business Club of America	www.latinbiz.net	business professional organization
Latino Professional Network	www.lponline.com	association of Latino professionals and students in a variety of professions

SEGMENT	SITE	TARGET AUDIENCE
Professional Organizations (cont.)		
National Association of Hispanic Federal Executive	www.nahfe.org	Organization of Hispanics who work for the federal government
National Hispanic Business Association	www.nhba.org	National organization of students and alumni interested in education and business issues for Hispanics
National Hispanic Real Estate Professionals	www.nahrep.org	real estate professionals
National Hispanic Corporate Council	www.nhcc-hq.org	information on Hispanic, primarily for Fortune 1000 companies
National Hispanic Employee Association	www.nhea.org	professional organization
National Latino Communication Center	www.nlcc.com	professional organization
National Society of Hispanic MBA's	www.nshmba.org	professional organization for Hispanic MBAs
Professional Hispanics in Energy	www.phie.org	professional organization
Society of Hispanic Professional Engineers	www.shpe.org	professional organization for Hispanic engineers
The National Association of Hispanic Journalists	www.nahj.org	professional organization for Hispanic journalists
National Association of Hispanic professionals	www.nshp.org	network organization for Hispanic professionals
Hispanic Entrepreneurs	www.hispanic-net.org	Hispanic professionals
National Hispanic Leadership Institute	www.nhli.org	Hispanic leadership
National Society for Hispanic professionals	www.nshp.com	Hispanic professionals
Hispanics in Philanthropy	www.hip.com	Hispanics in philanthropy
Hispanics in Maketing101	www.hm101.com	Hispanics in marketing
The Hispanic Association on Corporate Responsibility	www.Hacr.org	Hispanics in working with corporate CEOs
New America Alliance	www.naaonline.org	Hispanic investor group
U.S. Hispanic Chamber of Commerce	www.USHCC.org	Hispanic business association
The National Association of Hispanic Journalists	www.NAHJ.com	Hispanic journalists
Search Engines		
Las Culturas	www.lasculturas.com	links to many sites that offer information on a variety of topics
Latin World	www.latinworld.com	Spanish and English site with lots of links
Latin Index	www.latinindex.com	In Spanish with links country by country

Index